THE
ARTISANAL
KITCHEN

PARTY
FOOD

ARTISAN
KITCHEN

PARTY FOOD

GO-TO RECIPES
for **COCKTAIL PARTIES,**
BUFFETS, SIT-DOWN DINNERS,
and **HOLIDAY FEASTS**

SUSAN SPUNGEN

ARTISAN | NEW YORK

CONTENTS

-5-
SIT-DOWN DINNERS
72

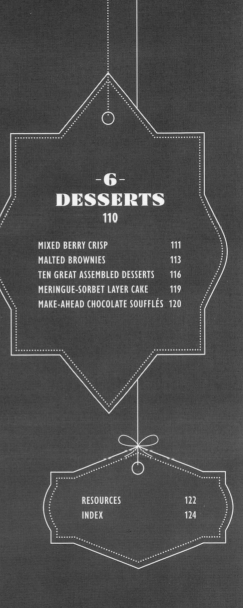

-6-
DESSERTS
110

HOSTING WITH EASE

A gifted host makes it look easy. He or she knows the shortcuts that make entertaining less laborious and more enjoyable for everyone. Some of us were raised by such a person, but if these skills skipped a generation, this book will help you look as though you learned it all as a child.

A HOST'S FOUR GOLDEN RULES

1. CODDLE YOUR GUESTS. Make them feel comfortable and welcome. Be hyperthoughtful: make a guest's favorite dessert; provide comfy, inexpensive Chinese slippers to wear indoors on a wintry evening; or use the tableware that was a gift from the guests. Let people know you're thinking about them.

2. PLAN AHEAD. A realistic plan is the key to success. Choose a menu with dishes that can be prepared ahead of time, leaving only the simplest tasks—like heating a dish, cooking pasta or rice, or dressing a salad—for the last minute. Your goal should be to have as little sweat on your brow (and mess in the kitchen) as possible when the doorbell rings.

3. LESS CAN BE MORE. A few beautiful, well-conceived, and well-prepared dishes will go over big. If you have to make a million different things, something—or everything—will suffer. If you drive yourself to the edge of sanity in preparing the food and cleaning the house, you'll feel like collapsing by the time your guests arrive. Keep it simple, and you'll be ready when it's time to have fun.

4. WHEN THE PARTY STARTS, BE IN IT. If you are running around frantically, with your guests asking, "Are you *sure* there's nothing I can do?," who can relax? You want to enjoy the party with your guests. They came to see you, and a good host is present and engaged.

HOW TO PLAN A MENU

The goal is to get the maximum impact for the least amount of work, or at least figure out how to streamline the work, spreading it over several days, so you aren't going crazy at the last minute. Trial and error is the best way to learn what not to do, but you will find an example of a successful menu at the start of each recipe chapter.

THREE LISTS YOU CAN'T LIVE WITHOUT

Spending a few minutes making lists will save you immeasurable time, not to mention stress, later on. Put a little box next to each item so you can have the satisfaction of checking it off as you accomplish each task. In the end, even if you don't refer back to the lists frequently, the act of making them will help you organize your thoughts and stay focused.

1. THE GUEST LIST. Strive for a "mixer": instead of inviting a group of people who all know one another well, mix it up a bit and invite friends and acquaintances who may not know one another well, or at all. It's always nice if a guest knows someone, and he or she will know you, the host. Unless the party is an intimate affair, be a bit of a matchmaker, and try to bring together people who you think have things in common and who will enjoy meeting one another. You'll be surprised at how seemingly disparate friends will find common ground.

2. THE SHOPPING LIST. Try to get everything you'll need for cooking, except for perishable foods like salad greens, all at once, so you can spend your time in the kitchen, not running out for forgotten ingredients. Divide your master shopping list by sections of the store—dairy, meat, fish, grocery, produce—or by different stores if you need to make more than one stop for groceries. Add additional list sections for liquor and wine, other party supplies, and flowers.

3. THE PREP LIST. Break your planning down into a list of tasks, day by day, and put them in order as best you can. What can you make ahead of time? Plan to get those jobs done early, so you can cross them off the list. Seeing everything on paper will give you a more realistic view of what you can accomplish, too, and whether you're being overly ambitious.

At the end of each day, revise the list as you cross some things off and get more detailed about the tasks still remaining. For the "day of" list, order the jobs chronologically with the first things first and the tasks you need to do just before your guests arrive last.

INVITATIONS

Invitations should convey the who, what, when, and where of your event and evoke the tone of the party. From engraved to e-mailed, the invitation should embody the formality—or dress code—of the occasion. Throwing a ladies' lunch? Go for something classic and comfortable, like stationery engraved with your initials. Hosting a potluck for coworkers? An e-mailed invitation means it's an easygoing affair. Try using a casual, colorful electronic invitation for a big birthday bash. That way friends and relatives can keep track of who is coming, helping to build anticipation for the event.

HOW TO TIME AN INVITATION

Whether you're mailing invitations or inviting guests by phone, timing is key. Send an invitation too late and your friends may already be booked; send it too early and it might be misplaced or forgotten. The following advice should serve as a guideline for various occasions. Use your best judgment for your specific event.

EVENT	INVITATION LEAD TIME
Anniversary party	3 to 6 weeks before the event
Birthday party	3 weeks
Casual party	Same day to 2 weeks
Christmas party	1 month
Cocktail party	1 to 4 weeks
Formal dinner	3 to 6 weeks
Graduation party	3 weeks
Housewarming party	1 to 3 weeks
Informal dinner	1 to 3 weeks
Lunch or tea	Last minute to 2 weeks
Thanksgiving dinner	6 to 8 weeks

HOW TO MAKE GUESTS MINGLE

Don't leave guests to awkwardly mingle at a party you're hosting. If it's a crowd filled with people who don't know one another, it's important to give people something to go on. When making introductions, try to jump-start the conversation—explain where you know each guest from, or bring up something they have in common—then break away once a conversation has been sparked.

HOW TO APPEAR CALM, COOL, AND COLLECTED

The art of hosting is making it look effortless; this is easiest for hosts who really love the pace and pressures of putting out a spread for friends. But even they know to ease this pace by planning parties for which most of the work can be done in advance.

The trickiest time is when your guests are arriving. You want to welcome them with open arms, but there are coats to put away, drinks to fetch, flowers to put in vases, and things in the kitchen to attend to. Keep your event running smoothly by making sure that your pre-party setup is complete before the first guests arrive. Transform anxiety into enthusiasm; both have an upbeat pace. Make a timeline for the evening in advance, mapping out when you'll clear the cocktail snacks, make last-minute sauces in the kitchen, let ice cream soften, open after-dinner drinks, et cetera. The timeline should be as detailed as possible, turning the evening into a well-choreographed dance. Preparedness helps make everything look effortless.

HOW TO CORRAL THE KIDS

When you invite children into your home, you're giving up some level of control. Make your peace ahead of time with the mess and the noise kids can make. If you haven't childproofed your home because your own toddler is a saint, be mindful that others might not be so placid. Hide the Swedish pottery, and place those carefully laid trays of nuts and olives out of reach. The clever host has kid-friendly snacks on hand and whips up Bambini Pasta (pasta with butter and grated Parmesan—the most universally appreciated dish among the younger set) for dinner. Don't be afraid to bribe kids: a fun dessert (preferably one that they can help decorate before serving) may help elicit their best behavior. Check with the parents first to see whether you might be able to let the kids watch a movie together in another room while the grown-ups have a leisurely meal. For larger parties, it may be worth it to hire a babysitter to watch the kids and keep them occupied. A word to the wise: Your own kids may be well behaved and enjoy asparagus, but you'll have to be very diplomatic about scolding your friends' children. Even if they're monsters, they're your guests, too.

TEN JOBS YOU CAN DELEGATE

Relinquish your grip on some of the busywork. Adult children, spouses, and friends can really come in handy with the chores below.

1. Setting the table
2. Ironing and folding napkins
3. Cleaning wineglasses that have been gathering dust on a distant shelf
4. Setting up the bar
5. Slicing lemon and lime wedges for drinks
6. Buying ice and making ice buckets for the bar
7. Preparing water carafes
8. Slicing bread
9. Opening wine
10. Lighting candles

TAKE FIVE

Schedule a small break in the action about an hour before your guests are due so you can change your clothes and perhaps wash the flour out of your hair. Chances are you'll be busy up to the last minute, but if you schedule a break, you can make sure you're not wearing your cooking sweats when guests arrive. It's okay to still be calmly fiddling in the kitchen at party time, but you want to be fresh and ready to greet guests.

TIMING IS EVERYTHING

An inability to coordinate the timing of a meal can be the downfall of even the best cooks. We've all been to (or thrown) a dinner party where the main course didn't manage to make it to the table until eleven o'clock, or half the guests had finished their ravioli by the time the poor host got to sit down and join them. Getting all the components of a meal on the table at the same time, and at their peak flavor and temperature, requires levelheaded multitasking, which is impossible without good planning. Timing should be on your mind from the get-go: when designing the menu, choose dishes that won't collide in the oven or on the stove, and balance items that require last-minute touches with those that can be made completely ahead of time.

THINKING BACKWARD

When planning how to finish your tasks, make a list starting with the ones that must be done at the last minute, and work backward to those for which the timing is not as crucial. Make your list with the do-aheads at the top and the crucial items at the very bottom. This way, you'll have ample time for the last-minute jobs.

For example, some dishes are better the next day, such as a braise that you want to let cool so you can skim the fat from the top before reheating and serving it. If you're baking a dessert, in most cases you will be able to get that out of the way the night before or first thing the morning of the party. When you write your menu, make sure to choose a few items that can (or must) be cooked ahead, and save as little as possible for the last minute. Allow yourself a time cushion for those little tasks that always seem to come up right before your guests ring the doorbell.

DON'T DRINK AND HOST

Once your guests have arrived, of course, it's fine to sip some wine, and once the meal has been served, relax and have a couple of glasses. But when there are still guests to seat and cooking to be done and your nerves are acting up, a cocktail is not the cure. It will only result in more chaos and, possibly, last-minute blunders that can ruin hours of hard work.

HOW TO SURVIVE CRUNCH TIME

The few hours before a party—when you're cooking up a storm and hiding your slippers under the bed—can (or should) be a bit like a ballet. Try to choreograph your movements by planning ahead so you can keep your cool. Don't get overwhelmed, and prioritize when time is running short. Nervous cooks sometimes make too much ahead of time, for fear that everything won't come out at the same time. Cooking ahead is recommended, but some things simply must be done *à la minute*, or at the last minute. Precooked pasta will be a gummy mess, for example, and delicate fish fillets will probably fall apart and/or dry out if you have to reheat them.

Anything that must be green and crisp, like green vegetables or a salad, should be saved for last. If you're steaming vegetables, prepare them and place them (and the water) in a steamer on the stove, but don't turn on the heat until you are almost ready to serve. Wash the greens and prepare the components for the salad (including the dressing), and even refrigerate them in the bowl you are going to serve in, but don't dress or toss the salad in advance.

Remember that all meat needs to rest after coming out of the oven, so plan to do other last-minute preparations during those 15 minutes or so. If you are serving something that must be eaten immediately, hot off the grill or the stove, make sure all the other components of the meal are completed first.

SIX WORTHY INVESTMENTS

If you have the space to store them, having these items on hand will make entertaining so much easier, even if you use them only once a year.

1. CASE OF WINEGLASSES (USUALLY 36 TO A BOX). Choose an all-purpose shape that can be used for red wine, white wine, or even soft drinks, and buy them cheaply at a restaurant supply store. Store them in the box they came in (they will need to be washed before using) or, better, in a plastic caddy specifically designed for the purpose that will keep them clean between uses.

2. CLOTH NAPKINS. Go with standard-issue restaurant ware; just aim for 100 percent cotton, since synthetic blends don't feel very nice against the skin, nor do they absorb liquids very well. Store clean, folded napkins in giant resealable plastic bags, so they're ready for use.

3. TABLE LINENS. These don't have to break the bank. Have on hand a few sturdy tablecloths, in sizes that cover your dining table and any other tables that you can press into service for a party, such as your kitchen table. White tablecloths are nice, but darker colors or prints and damasks won't show the inevitable stains the way white will. Depending on your space, you may want cloths that reach the floor so you can stash extra supplies under the tables during your party.

4. EXTRA SERVING UTENSILS. If you like throwing buffet parties, you would be wise to invest in some extra-large serving spoons, ladles, spatulas, forks, and tongs that are attractive enough to be on the table. Too often, we use kitchen utensils that don't add much to the look of the table. Unwieldy serving utensils will also slow down your guests' progress through the buffet line. Try to choose implements that can be used easily with one hand, like scissor-style salad tongs, for instance, rather than a traditional two-piece salad server set. Stainless steel and wood are good choices and not too pricey.

5. LARGE PLATTERS AND SERVING BOWLS. Every host needs extra platters for party time. White platters are the best default since everything looks good on white, and it lets the food shine. Go for a variety of sizes and shapes. These can become a decorative element in your home when not in use if you devote a wall of shelves or a glass-front cabinet to their storage.

6. CHAFING DISHES. A chafing dish is really the only way to keep food warm for an extended period of time. Chafing dishes are essential for buffet parties, cocktail parties, and stations, especially when your party is outdoors. There are many new and sleek chafing dishes for the modern host that won't call attention to themselves. Look for ones with clean lines and without a lot of unnecessary ornamental curlicues. At the same time, you don't want them to look as if they belong in the high-school cafeteria, either. Choose chafing dishes that go with your serving pieces and your decor.

TEN KITCHEN MUST-HAVES

Aside from the usual *batterie de cuisine*, here are a few things that every successful host should have in his or her kitchen arsenal.

1. CAST-IRON SKILLET. For searing and roasting meat, poultry, and fish, or making corn bread, crumbles, and cobblers that can be brought right to the table for a rustic presentation, cast iron is probably the best all-purpose pan around. If you like making desserts in a skillet, it's a good idea to reserve one for that purpose only, so your strawberry crisp doesn't taste like salmon.

2. ENAMELED DUTCH OVEN. This oven-to-table staple is for braising meat stews, short ribs, or pork shoulders, or making a hearty soup. Available in an array of stylish colors, this is a pricey item but one that will last a lifetime and lend a rustic beauty to your table. Enameled cast iron will retain its heat for a long time, which is a big plus for serving cold-weather meals.

3. IMMERSION BLENDER. This is best for pureeing soups and sauces right in the pot, or blending a small batch of salad dressing. If you get one with a whisk attachment, you'll be able to make whipped cream quickly right before serving dessert.

4. GRATIN DISHES. Simple, attractive, oven-to-table baking dishes are wonderful for buffets or family-style meals. Cooking a dish in its serving vessel means one less thing to platter up at crunch time, and it keeps the food warm, too.

5. KITCHEN TONGS. A comfortable pair of tongs will make you a faster and more facile cook. Tongs are not to be used for the most delicate items, like fish, but they should be an extension of your hand for just about everything else.

6. FISH SPATULA. This long, thin, angled spatula is a must for releasing and turning delicate fish fillets when pan-searing.

7. INSTANT-READ THERMOMETER. You shouldn't be without this tiny and inexpensive tool. It will save you a lot of stress and will prevent your having to apologize for overcooked (or undercooked) meat, poultry, and fish.

8. OFFSET SPATULA. These come in a variety of sizes, but I like the smallest ones best, since they do most jobs well. An offset spatula is absolutely necessary for icing a cake or spreading anything and is convenient for turning small items like blini or even removing a delicate cookie from a baking sheet.

9. MICROPLANE GRATER. This versatile tool is perfect for finely grating nutmeg, lemon zest, and especially Parmesan cheese, which resembles freshly fallen snow when grated with a Microplane and sprinkled over pasta or salad.

10. JAPANESE MANDOLINE. This handy item is inexpensive and is indispensable for making paper-thin slices of apples, fennel, radishes, carrots, raw mushrooms, Parmesan cheese, and anything else that's firm and sliceable, for salads and garnishes. It's also indispensable for thinly slicing potatoes for a gratin.

-2-

SETTING THE SCENE

Taking the time to get your place party-ready is important in the overall impression that is made on your guests. You can create the mood you want by making considered choices when it comes to lighting, decoration, and a host of other details that all add up to a personal statement. Make choices that are right for your guests, being as formal or informal as you like.

HOW TO ARRANGE YOUR SPACE

Whether your place is small or large, it's important to consider how people will be moving through the room(s): where they'll congregate, sit, stand, and linger. The key is to get people to spread out and keep moving as much as possible. If you've entertained before, you have some idea of where the bottlenecks naturally occur, so you have a head start on trying to prevent and avoid them. Place a large table in a central space away from any known bottlenecks. Remove the chairs from around the table and spread them throughout the house to give guests another place to sit and to provide easier access to the food. Float the table in the middle of a room rather than push it up against a wall, to allow guests to get to it from all sides. Try drawing a simple floor plan to see how your furniture might be arranged to create a good flow. Even if your drawing is not to scale, it's helpful to visualize the arrangement in two dimensions. It will also provide a visual guide if you have helpers assisting with the setup.

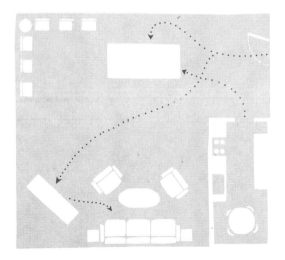

WHERE'S THE BAR?

Since the bar, like the snacks, will attract loiterers, it should be placed in an open, central location, away from high-traffic areas such as doorways and hallways or any narrow spaces around furniture. Placing the bar in a part of your home that tends to have less traffic during a party will draw your guests there and help prevent traffic jams. Of course, you don't want it so far out of the way that it's isolated from other rooms, if you're hoping for people to spread out. It should also be convenient for you to replenish it. If you are planning a really large party (more than thirty people), consider a second bar, or a service bar behind the scenes from which drinks can be served to guests from trays.

HOW TO USE STATIONS

Caterers create food stations for the flexibility they offer, and they come in handy for the amateur host as well. Creating stations, especially for a grazing cocktail party, means you spread the food out into distinct areas, say, with crudités and dips on a table in one room and sushi in another (or whatever type of station your heart desires). Stations make a party fun to explore and encourage guests to keep moving to different corners of your space, with the added benefit that they encounter new people to chat with. This keeps the traffic jams to a minimum. Stations also allow you to create mini themes, menu-wise. Each station should be self-sufficient, with all the accoutrements and utensils at hand.

A PLACE-SETTING CHEAT SHEET

Below are some basic table-setting rules. Think of each setting as a block of marble, to be chiseled away as the meal goes on. As we use our utensils and they are cleared from the table, the setting shrinks, from the outside in, until the final course is served.

· Forks to the left, knives to the right of the plate.

· Spoons on the right, with the knives.

· The silverware will be used from the outside in, so if you are serving a salad first, the salad fork should be the outermost utensil, and the next one in should be the one that will be used next—probably a large fork for the main course. If you are starting with soup, the soupspoon should be placed to the right of the knives.

· The napkin can be placed to the left of the plate, with the forks on it, or on the charger.

· The butter dish goes in the left-hand corner. If you have proper butter knives (which are small and short), they should be placed across the butter dishes. If you are using a regular knife for butter, place it to the right of the plate, on the outside, if the butter will be served at the beginning of the meal.

· Dessert utensils can be placed at the top of the setting, over the plate, or brought out when that course is served. It is customary to bring a fork and a spoon, unless the dessert can be eaten with only a spoon (for example, if you're serving pudding).

· The glasses go in the right-hand corner, starting with the water glass, which should be just above the knives.

· Wineglasses should be placed to the right of the water glass, in the order in which they will be used. So, if you're starting with white wine and then moving on to red, your glasses would be in this order, from left to right: water glass, white-wine glass, red-wine glass. They can also be arranged in

a triangle, still with the water glass above the knife, and the first wineglass just to the right of it. If there is a second wineglass, place it behind those two.

- After-dinner glasses can be brought to the table at the end of the meal. If you are serving dessert wine, bring the glasses out with dessert.

- Coffee mugs or teacups should be brought to the table (or the living room, if your party migrates) with dessert. At a more casual party, you might ask how many of your guests would like to have one or the other. Teacups should be on saucers, with spoons for stirring in sugar.

WHAT KIND OF WINEGLASSES DO I NEED?

Here are the basics: The wider the mouth of the glass, the greater the effect on the wine of oxygen, which "relaxes" the flavors and brings the aroma out. Generally, this effect is more desirable with red wines and full-bodied whites, like chardonnay. White-wine glasses have a narrower opening, and red-wine glasses are more round. (Rosé is traditionally drunk out of a tulip-shaped glass, but a white-wine glass is perfectly acceptable.) At a formal dinner, different wines would be served in different glasses, even if both wines are reds or whites.

Though there is a specific shape for every type of wine, using one glass for red and one for white would suffice. If you don't have the storage space or budget for two sets, then look for a glass with a shape that accommodates any type of wine. It should be big enough for red, but not so balloon-shaped that it can't work for a white. Rinse your guests' glasses before refilling them with a new wine.

TO SHAKE OR TO PINCH

If you're serving kosher salt or regular-to-fine sea salt, use a regular salt-shaker. But for flaky or coarse salt, only a little dish or bowl, also known as a saltcellar, will work, since the grains are too big to pass through the holes of a shaker. Using a saltcellar means you'll be faced with the finger conundrum. With good friends or family, you may not mind letting your guests use their fingers to pinch some salt for their plates, but you could also use a little spoon for scooping, especially if the crowd is not very intimate. If you have more than six people, particularly at a long table, put out two or more saltshakers, or dishes, for easy access. They don't necessarily have to match. If the occasion is formal, or if you happen to be a collector, you can provide a small dish or shaker for each person so there's no concern about using fingers.

SHOULD I PUT PEPPER ON THE TABLE?

If you're serving black pepper, it should be freshly ground. Banish the pre-ground stuff for cooking as well as at the table. A miniature pepper mill is a nice choice for the table, especially if you have a long table and want to put out a few. Another option is to grind the pepper yourself, right before the meal, and serve it in tiny bowls as you might serve salt and other seasonings, such as red pepper flakes. If the only grinder you have is not a good-looking one or one of those tall, showy grinders, this is the way to go.

LESS IS ALMOST ALWAYS MORE

A few well-placed pops of color, and perhaps some candles, are often all that's needed to make a room sparkle. As with your menu, let the season be your guide, and bring some of the outdoors in. A few flowering branches are dramatic in the spring, unusual pumpkins and squashes are great in the fall, and simple greenery for the holidays is all you need to dress up your space.

IN PRAISE OF THE DIMMER SWITCH

Soft lighting creates a warm and cozy evening atmosphere and flatters your guests, your home, and the food. A multitude of sins can be easily overlooked when people are basking in a warm glow. Create even more of a mood with candles (or go romantic and use *only* candles; if you use several there will be enough light, and you will be surprised at how quickly eyes adjust to low light). If you don't have dimmers, use 40-watt lightbulbs and play with the placement of lamps so the light isn't direct.

FIVE WAYS TO DECORATE WITHOUT FLOWERS

1. FRUITS AND VEGETABLES. A big bowl of peaches or tomatoes in August will evoke the season in a beautiful way. Gourds and small pumpkins in the fall will last for months. Decorative kale or cabbage in pretty pots looks great in the fall, too.

2. POTTED PLANTS. Mini daffodils in the spring are charming: pop the plastic pots they come in into a slightly larger terra-cotta pot. Orchids are beautiful placed around a room or on the table. Fresh potted herbs in spring and summer are a lovely and fragrant way to decorate the table; combine a few different types in small pots in clusters on the table. Mini evergreens look festive around the Christmas holidays.

3. FOLIAGE AND GREENERY. These cost less and last longer than flowers. Think of using large leaves in a tall container placed on the floor, or plant wheatgrass in a simple container; it takes only a few days to grow, and it looks fresh and modern.

4. BRANCHES. A wholesale flower market is a great place to find beautiful, decorative branches, including large ones that can be placed in a big pot on the floor or in an entryway. This is an excellent way to bring a little nature indoors without ever having to worry about watering or sunlight.

5. EUCALYPTUS. As a centerpiece, eucalyptus is far too fragrant, but it's perfect in the bathroom or a bedroom, and can be found at farmers' markets and flower shops in the fall. Even after the branches and leaves dry out, they're pretty and decorative.

HOW TO BE YOUR OWN FLORIST

If you live in a big city, locate a wholesale flower market and find out whether individual vendors sell to the public. Many do, and most likely you'll have to pay in cash. The flowers are less expensive and often fresher. That longevity will allow you to create your arrangements a day or two ahead of time. If you don't have access to a flower market, buy what's freshest from the local grocer or farmers' market. Choose individual bunches of a single type of bloom so you can mix and match as you want. Of course, if it's the right time of year, and you have a garden or a good friend who does, take full advantage of that.

NO VASE? NO PROBLEM

Any container can be used to hold an arrangement, as long as it's watertight. Nontraditional vessels add a lot of charm. Keep your eyes peeled at flea markets and tag sales. An old pitcher could become your favorite vase. Here are a few great alternatives to the typical glass vase.

- Canning jars
- Teapots and pitchers
- Glass bottles
- Bowls
- Pumpkins
- Coffee cans or old jars
- Containers inside paper bags
- French flower cans or galvanized buckets
- Ice buckets

3

HORS D'OEUVRES

When you are brainstorming about assembled hors d'oeuvres, begin with the vehicle—a piece of toast, a hollowed-out cherry tomato—and build from there. The ingredients that get piled on top of or into your base don't have to be fancy to make for a sophisticated spread. In addition to a few composed hors d'oeuvres, you can offer a cheese plate, a salumi plate, or a crudités platter along with some nuts, olives, dips, crackers, and flatbreads. Depending on the size of your party and how long you expect people to stay, you might want to offer all these options, or just some cheese and bread to nibble on. Whatever you decide, remember that less is often more, and resist the urge to overdo. Leave yourself some time to make the offerings look beautiful, plentiful, and inviting.

TRY THIS MENU

WHITE BEAN AND TOMATO TOASTS (PAGE 33)

CLASSIC SHRIMP COCKTAIL

CHERRY TOMATOES STUFFED WITH HUMMUS (SEE PAGE 37)

SMOKED SALMON CANAPÉS

ARANCINI (RICE BALLS)

CRAB SHIU MAI

WHY IT WORKS

This menu is focused on self-contained items. All can be eaten in one or two bites, and sauces, if any, are thick enough so that guests won't fear getting drips down their clothing.

GOUGÈRES

This is a very versatile recipe in terms of timing. You can make the gougères and serve them right away, or pipe out the batter and freeze on a baking sheet before transferring to a resealable plastic bag and storing in the freezer until ready to bake. You can also bake them right away, then cool and freeze them to be rewarmed before serving. Whichever method you choose, make an effort to serve these classic cheese puffs warm; they are irresistible with wine or cocktails. Change the flavor with different cheeses—the choice is yours—just keep the amount the same.

6 TABLESPOONS UNSALTED BUTTER, CUT INTO PATS

½ TEASPOON COARSE SALT

1 CUP FLOUR

4 EGGS

FRESHLY GRATED NUTMEG

CAYENNE PEPPER

1 CUP GRATED GRUYÈRE, PLUS MORE FOR SPRINKLING (OPTIONAL)

If baking right away, preheat the oven to 400°F. Line two baking sheets with parchment or silicone baking mats.

Combine 1 cup water, the butter, and the salt in a small saucepan. Bring to a boil. As soon as the butter melts, add the flour, all at once.

Stir over low heat until a smooth dough forms and a film starts to form on the bottom of the pan, about 2 minutes.

Transfer to a stand mixer fitted with the paddle attachment and beat for a minute or so to cool the mixture slightly.

continued

Beat in the eggs, one at a time, making sure each one is completely incorporated before adding the next (you can also add the eggs by hand; it will just take a bit of muscle).

Add a dash of nutmeg, a pinch of cayenne, and the 1 cup Gruyère and beat to combine.

Transfer to a piping bag fitted with a large plain tip and pipe out the mixture into small mounds on the baking sheets, about the size of a cherry tomato, about 2 inches apart. Sprinkle with more grated cheese, if desired, and bake for 20 to 25 minutes, until golden and puffed and not too moist inside (or they may collapse). Let cool in the oven for 5 minutes with the heat off and the door ajar. Serve immediately, or cool and freeze and then reheat in a 350° oven before serving.

WHITE BEAN AND TOMATO TOASTS

SERVES 8 TO 10

This easy (and inexpensive) hors d'oeuvre is a variation on a classic Spanish tapa, *pan con tomate*, in which toasted bread is rubbed with garlic and a halved ripe tomato so that the tomato softens the crunchy exterior of the bread. Here a white-bean puree is added. The puree can be made one or two days ahead and kept in the fridge. Make sure to let it come to room temperature before serving.

1 CRUSTY BAGUETTE

1 TOMATO

2 TABLESPOONS EXTRA-VIRGIN OLIVE OIL, PLUS MORE FOR SERVING

2 GARLIC CLOVES, 1 CHOPPED AND 1 HALVED

ONE 15½-OUNCE CAN WHITE BEANS, DRAINED AND RINSED

½ TEASPOON COARSE SALT

FRESHLY GROUND BLACK PEPPER

1 TABLESPOON RED OR WHITE WINE VINEGAR

Position a rack in the middle of the oven and preheat the oven to 375°F.

Slice the baguette into ¼-inch-thick slices. Spread the slices out on a large rimmed baking sheet and bake until the edges are golden, 7 to 10 minutes. Set aside.

Halve the tomato and chop one half into small pieces. Set the remaining half aside.

Heat the 2 tablespoons oil in a medium saucepan over medium heat. Add the chopped garlic clove and sauté until it begins to brown, about 3 minutes. Add the beans,

½ cup water, the salt, and a dash of pepper, bring to a simmer, and cook until most of the liquid has evaporated, about 5 minutes. Add the vinegar and mash the beans with a fork until roughly pureed. Remove from the heat.

Rub the slices of bread with the halved garlic clove and then with the cut side of the remaining half tomato. Spoon about 1 tablespoon of the bean puree onto each slice and top with the chopped tomato. Drizzle with extra-virgin olive oil and serve.

GUACAMOLE

One thing that is always better when homemade is guacamole. We all know that avocados brown quickly, so any store-bought version will be full of preservatives and won't have the fresh, pure flavor of homemade. Guacamole is super simple to make, and it will keep for several hours in the fridge if necessary, even if you have to scrape the top before serving to remove any browning that might have occurred. If you have a *molcajete*, the traditional lava-rock mortar and pestle that is common in Mexico and Mexican restaurants, use it to both make and serve the guac.

1 SMALL WHITE ONION, FINELY MINCED

1 MEDIUM JALAPEÑO, CORED, SEEDED, AND FINELY CHOPPED, PLUS MORE TO TASTE

¼ CUP CHOPPED FRESH CILANTRO

1½ TEASPOONS COARSE SALT, PLUS MORE TO TASTE

3 RIPE AVOCADOS

JUICE OF ½ LIME, PLUS MORE TO TASTE

1 MEDIUM TOMATO, SEEDED AND CHOPPED

TORTILLA CHIPS, FOR SERVING

In a medium bowl or *molcajete*, combine the onion, jalapeño, cilantro, and salt. Mix well, using a wooden spoon to combine thoroughly.

Cut the avocados in half lengthwise and remove and discard the pits. Remove the flesh and add to the other ingredients in the bowl.

Use a large fork to mash the avocado, leaving some texture. Add the lime juice and tomato to the mixture. Adjust the seasonings with salt, lime juice, and jalapeño, and serve with tortilla chips.

TEN QUICK HORS D'OEUVRES

1. Belgian endive petals with fresh fig, goat cheese, and chopped walnuts

2. Thick-cut potato chips with crème fraîche, smoked salmon, and dill

3. Cucumber cups with lime mayo and lump crabmeat, garnished with chile powder

4. Cherry tomatoes stuffed with hummus and topped with olive slivers

5. Toasted baguette topped with fresh mozzarella, cherry tomato, and pesto (can be served warm and melty or at room temperature)

6. Celery boats filled with lemon mayo, Italian oil-packed tuna, and capers

7. Party rye triangles (toasted) with fresh turkey, herb mayo, and cranberry chutney

8. Melon balls or chunks wrapped with prosciutto

9. Wheat crackers topped with creamy pâté and sliced cornichon

10. Tortilla chips with guacamole and cooked shrimp, garnished with cilantro or salsa

CRUDITÉS: HOW TO CLASS UP AN OLD STANDBY

Choose your veggies wisely, and make the tiny bit of effort to peel and cut regular carrots, rather than buy a bag of "baby" ones. By doing so, you've already classed up this old standby considerably. Browse the vegetable aisle for crunchy produce that appeals to you and makes for a variety of colors and flavors. Some great options are fennel, endive, colorful bell peppers, cucumbers (if you can find the seedless or "Persian" variety, they'll stay crunchy longer), asparagus spears, radishes, and summer squash. When it comes to presentation, experiment a little, making sure each spear or slice is easily accessible (you don't want to encourage more hands touching food than is necessary). Try standing the vegetables upright in glasses or glass jars, or offering a few different compatible dips.

CRUDITÉS WITH GORGONZOLA DIP

Everyone loves their vegetables with a little fat. A crudités platter (see opposite) should be full of beautiful, crunchy, fresh veggies, which will do double duty as vehicles for a thick, creamy, tangy dip. This one's a real winner.

¾ CUP BUTTERMILK OR PLAIN YOGURT DRINK

½ CUP MAYONNAISE

¼ CUP PLAIN LOW-FAT YOGURT

1 TEASPOON WHITE WINE VINEGAR

2 SCALLIONS, SLICED

6 OUNCES GORGONZOLA, CRUMBLED

COARSE SALT AND FRESHLY GROUND BLACK PEPPER

FRESHLY CUT AND TRIMMED VEGETABLES, SUCH AS BELL PEPPERS, CARROTS, ASPARAGUS, AND SNAP PEAS (SEE OPPOSITE)

Whisk together the buttermilk or yogurt drink, mayonnaise, yogurt, vinegar, and scallions in a bowl.

Stir in the Gorgonzola and season to taste with salt and pepper.

Refrigerate until ready to serve. The dip will keep, covered in the refrigerator, for 2 to 3 days. Serve with the vegetables.

THE CHEESE CHART: CHOOSING BY CATEGORY

When putting together a cheese plate or platter, the key is balance. The specifics should reflect your personal taste, but be sure to present a variety of types of cheese—one that's hard and salty, another that's soft and buttery, and one that's more forward: stinky or tangy. Even if you strongly favor one style, try not to double up on any of the categories below. This way, there's something for everyone.

HARD CHEESE
PARMIGIANO-REGGIANO, AGED GOUDA
Hard cheeses are often grated, but for a cheese plate, they can be chiseled into bite-size chunks. Hard cheeses tend to be salty and granular and go well with honey and dried fruit.

FIRM CHEESE
MANCHEGO, CHEDDAR, COMTÉ, GRUYÈRE, JARLSBERG
The longer a cheese is aged, the firmer it will be. Firm cheeses are ideal for slicing, so this category includes many sandwich favorites, but they deserve to be rediscovered in their own right on your grazing buffet.

SEMISOFT CHEESE
MORBIER, FONTINA, MUENSTER, PROVOLONE, EMMENTHAL
These are good melting cheeses, with a consistency that falls between those of spreadable and grating cheeses. It's important to serve them at room temperature so their creaminess can be appreciated.

FRESH CHEESE
RICOTTA, MOZZARELLA, CHÈVRE, BOURSIN
Because they haven't aged, these cheeses are mild and moist. A fresh cheese can be a great counterpoint to stronger flavors, and can also be embellished with herbs for a simple spread.

continued

BLOOMY CHEESE
BRIE, CAMEMBERT, ROBIOLA

These are cheeses with white rinds (formed from a mold growth that is completely edible) and rich, creamy interiors.

WASHED-RIND CHEESE
TALEGGIO, TOMME DE SAVOIE, ÉPOISSES, LIVAROT

Unlike the white rinds of bloomy cheeses, washed rinds are orange or brown from being bathed with beer, brine, brandy, or other liquids that encourage bacteria to grow. The process, unsurprisingly, makes for stinky cheese, but the insides are often creamy, if forward.

BLUE CHEESE
STILTON, GORGONZOLA, ROQUEFORT, CABRALES, MAYTAG BLUE

The blue mold that runs in "veins" throughout these crumbly, pungent cheeses may turn off the faint of heart, but the funky, salty flavor is more loved than not—at least by adults.

CHEESE STRAWS

This is an easy recipe that every host should have in his or her repertoire. Store-bought puff pastry makes it simple, and you can vary the flavors by adding different cheeses, spices, herbs, or even sesame or poppy seeds to the mix.

ONE 11-OUNCE SHEET THAWED
FROZEN PUFF PASTRY

1 EGG, BEATEN WITH
1 TABLESPOON WATER

1 CUP FRESHLY GRATED
PARMIGIANO-REGGIANO

1 TABLESPOON CHOPPED
FRESH ROSEMARY

Roll out the puff pastry on a floured surface to an even rectangle roughly 11 by 15 inches. Brush it with the egg wash. Sprinkle the Parmigiano-Reggiano and rosemary over the surface, and roll over the pastry with the rolling pin just to press the toppings into it.

Use a pizza cutter or a knife to cut the pastry lengthwise into ½-inch-wide strips. Transfer 6 strips to each of four parchment-lined baking sheets, twisting each strip into a tight spiral and placing the strips 1½ inches apart. Chill the straws until they're firm, about 15 minutes.

Preheat the oven to 400°F.

Bake the straws two sheets at a time for about 10 minutes, rotate the trays, and continue to bake for an additional 18 to 20 minutes, or until golden and crisp. Repeat with the remaining two trays.

SERVING
CHARCUTERIE AND SALUMI

A selection of cured meats is the perfect accompaniment to wine and cheese. Both charcuterie (French) and salumi (Italian) refer generally to cured meats, and pork usually plays a big role. Salumi, such as prosciutto, salami, and speck, are very popular choices, as are the slightly more formal liver pâtés and terrines.

SHOPPING FOR CURED MEATS

If there's a good gourmet shop in town—or an old-school deli in an Italian neighborhood that sells imported salumi—you're set. Ask for tastes, and get a few things you like, making sure there's a variety. For example, a bit of spicy soppressata; a smoked meat, like speck; some prosciutto, because everyone loves it; and maybe a non-pork item, like bresaola, which is cured lean beef.

If you don't have access to top-notch imported meats, don't fret. Remember, these delicacies wouldn't exist but for the need to preserve food; they travel well and can be ordered online (see Resources). You may want to buy a few whole salamis, which you can slice yourself (the slices needn't be paper-thin), or if it is sliced, be sure to order the meat vacuum-sealed and have it sent overnight so it doesn't dry out on its way to you.

continued

HOW TO PRESENT
CHARCUTERIE OR SALUMI

Cured meats are crowd-pleasers, and people will be glad to see them. It doesn't take much to make the distinction between good salami or ham and the kind of cold cuts your guests might remember from the processed lunch meats back in the day. Buy your salumi as close to party time as possible, so the flavor is at its peak. Some meats, like prosciutto and bresaola, will dry out quickly; fattier meats, like salami, will keep longer. In any case, make sure to handle them while they are well chilled; the slices will be easier to arrange when cold. Just be sure to serve at room temperature.

With thinly sliced salumi, like prosciutto, take care to overlap (rather than stack), folding each slice so guests can easily pick it up. Arrange the folded slices of meat in groups, so that it's easy to see what is on offer. Use a cutting board or even a stone or marble slab; that sort of presentation is a little more interesting than a plain white plate, and it's perfectly in keeping with the rustic origins of the food. If you are serving any whole, hard salami, serve it on a wood cutting board and cut several rounds when you set the board out, so your guests will be encouraged to eat it and cut more. You can prepare the platter or board a few hours in advance and return it to the fridge, lightly covered in plastic wrap; remove it an hour before serving. Good salumi needs little accompaniment, but some good bread, olives, and crisp fennel slices will go nicely.

PISSALADIÈRE

SERVES 8 TO 10

The best way to describe pissaladière is to say it is a French version of pizza, and it is the perfect accompaniment to drinks. Salty and warm, pissaladière fills the belly. It can easily be cut into bite-size pieces.

ONE 14-OUNCE SHEET FROZEN PUFF PASTRY OR 1-POUND PIECE OF FROZEN PIZZA DOUGH, THAWED (SEE NOTE)

1 EGG, LIGHTLY BEATEN

1 TABLESPOON EXTRA-VIRGIN OLIVE OIL

3 MEDIUM-SIZE SWEET ONIONS, HALVED AND THICKLY SLICED

1 TEASPOON FRESH THYME LEAVES

1 TEASPOON ANCHOVY PASTE (OPTIONAL)

COARSE SALT AND FRESHLY GROUND BLACK PEPPER

HEAPING ¼ CUP SLICED PITTED BLACK OLIVES

ABOUT 10 SLICED GRAPE TOMATOES

Roll out the puff pastry on a floured surface to an even thickness, roughly 12 by 15 inches. It should be a couple of inches larger than it was originally. Trim off a ½-inch strip of dough from all sides. Brush the edges sparingly with the egg, lay the strips of dough on top to make a crust around the border, and press gently. (Alternatively, stretch the pizza dough into an oval about 10 by 13 inches; let it rest briefly if it's too springy to hold its shape.)

Transfer the dough to a parchment-lined baking sheet and chill until needed.

Make caramelized onions: Heat the olive oil in a large skillet over high heat. Add the onions and cook, stirring occasionally, until they begin to brown, about 8 minutes.

Reduce the heat to low, add the thyme leaves and ¼ cup water, and continue cooking for about 10 minutes, or until the onions are meltingly soft.

continued

Add the anchovy paste, if using, and stir until completely combined.

Season the onions with salt and pepper and let cool. (The onions can be made up to 2 days ahead and kept in the refrigerator until ready to use.)

Preheat the oven to 400°F.

Use a fork to prick the pastry all over. Spread the caramelized onions evenly over the dough, then scatter the olives and tomatoes over the onions. Bake the pissaladière for 30 to 45 minutes, until it is uniformly golden brown and, if you're using puff pastry, has puffed up. Serve immediately.

NOTE
Thawing of pastry is best done overnight in the refrigerator, but pastry can also be left at room temperature until thawed, 1 or 2 hours.

PARMESAN PALMIERS

Even easier to make than cheese straws, palmiers are a variation on that theme: store-bought puff pastry is layered with cheese and herbs, and then rolled up toward the center into a kind of double-barreled log and baked. Slicing the log yields many individual bites with little effort, and palmiers keep well for several days.

ONE 14-OUNCE SHEET THAWED
FROZEN PUFF PASTRY

1 EGG, BEATEN WITH
1 TABLESPOON WATER

1½ CUPS FRESHLY GRATED
PARMIGIANO-REGGIANO

1 TABLESPOON PLUS 1 TEASPOON
FRESH THYME LEAVES

Roll out the pastry on a floured surface into an even rectangle a few inches larger than it was originally, roughly 12 by 15 inches. Brush the surface with the egg wash and sprinkle with 1 cup of the Parmigiano-Reggiano and the 1 tablespoon thyme leaves.

Starting at one of the long sides of the rectangle, roll the pastry up (not too tightly) like a jelly roll, stopping at the center, then roll it up from the other side to meet in the middle. Use a sharp knife to cut it into ¼-inch-wide slices (use your fingers to reshape any squashed pieces).

Place the palmiers 1 inch apart on a parchment-lined baking sheet. Brush them again with egg wash, then sprinkle with the remaining ½ cup Parmigiano-Reggiano and 1 teaspoon thyme leaves. Refrigerate for 30 minutes.

Preheat the oven to 400°F.

Bake the palmiers for 20 to 25 minutes, or until crisp and golden. Transfer to a cooling rack. When completely cool, store in an airtight container for 2 to 3 days.

GRAPE SCHIACCIATA

Schiacciata is an Italian regional variation on focaccia. In Tuscany, this delicious flatbread is often made with grapes during the wine grape harvest. This slightly unusual, not quite sweet or savory snack makes a rustic hors d'oeuvre to go with drinks.

EXTRA-VIRGIN OLIVE OIL

1-POUND PIECE OF THAWED FROZEN PIZZA DOUGH

COARSE SALT

1 TABLESPOON CHOPPED FRESH ROSEMARY

¾ CUP HALVED BLACK OR RED SEEDLESS GRAPES

Preheat the oven to 400°F and oil a baking sheet.

Stretch the dough into a rough oval about 10 by 13 inches. If the dough is too springy, let it rest for a few minutes and then try again. Drizzle the dough with olive oil and let it rest for 15 minutes.

Press your fingertips into the dough to make dimples all over the surface. Sprinkle with salt and the rosemary and scatter the grapes over it.

Bake the *schiacciata* for 30 minutes, or until the top is evenly golden and the bottom is browned and crisp. Cut into small pieces to serve.

4

BUFFETS

A buffet makes entertaining easier, whether a large group or a small one, especially if you don't have a lot of space at the table. A buffet will automatically invite your guests to make themselves at home, and with several dishes that guests can choose among and combine, everyone's dietary requirements can be met. An "open house" party—at which people come and go over the course of a few hours—naturally lends itself to a buffet, since the host is free from timing the courses.

Choose foods with staying power, such as a rice or grain salad, and avoid items that won't hold up well at room temperature. When serving meat, braises are a great idea, but avoid large cuts like a lamb shank, and opt for an easy-to-eat stew instead. Pasta is popular and easy for a buffet, but go for a baked pasta dish with a short shape that can be easily speared by a fork.

TRY THIS MENU

WILD RICE SALAD (PAGE 55)

RAW SHREDDED KALE SALAD

CARNITAS (PAGE 57)

BAKED ORECCHIETTE WITH SAUSAGE
AND BROCCOLI RABE (PAGE 63)

ROASTED VEGETABLES (SEE PAGES 103–104)

MIXED BERRY CRISP (PAGE 111)

WHY IT WORKS

This menu is made up of items that will look good and taste good even after sitting for a few hours on a buffet. They're easy to eat in small bites, too. Everything on this menu can be eaten with just a fork, which is essential for a party at which guests might be eating with their plates in their laps, or standing.

WILD RICE SALAD

This salad is great at room temperature, so it could become your famous potluck contribution, and it's also perfect for buffets. The salad is hearty but refreshing, thanks to some crunchy veggies and bright orange juice in the dressing. One of the best things about it is that you can prepare it almost completely in advance.

1½ TEASPOONS COARSE SALT

ONE 6-OUNCE PACKAGE PLAIN WILD RICE (1 CUP)

2 CUPS JASMINE RICE

1 CUP PECAN HALVES

JUICE OF 1 ORANGE

1 SHALLOT, MINCED

FRESHLY GROUND BLACK PEPPER

2 TABLESPOONS BALSAMIC OR RED WINE VINEGAR (OR A MIXTURE OF THE TWO)

½ CUP OLIVE OIL

1 CUCUMBER, PEELED AND CUT INTO ¼-INCH CUBES

1 RED BELL PEPPER, CORED, SEEDED, AND CUT INTO ¼-INCH CUBES

½ CUP DRIED CURRANTS OR CRANBERRIES

½ CUP CHOPPED FRESH FLAT-LEAF PARSLEY

2 TABLESPOONS RINSED CAPERS

Bring 4 cups water to a boil in a large saucepan. Add ½ teaspoon of the salt and the wild rice, reduce the heat, cover, and cook until about one-third of the grains have split but the rice is still slightly chewy, about 40 minutes. Drain well and transfer to a bowl to cool.

Meanwhile, combine the jasmine rice with 3 cups cold water and ½ teaspoon of the salt in a large saucepan and bring to a boil over high heat, then reduce to a simmer and cook, covered, until all of the liquid has been absorbed and the rice is tender, about 20 minutes. Turn off the heat and let sit, covered, for 5 minutes. Transfer the rice to a bowl to cool slightly, and fluff with a fork.

While the rice cooks, preheat the oven to 375°F.

Spread the pecans on a large rimmed baking sheet and toast in the oven, shaking the pan every few minutes so the nuts toast evenly and don't burn, about 8 minutes. Transfer them to a bowl. When they're cool enough to handle, break them lengthwise in half and set aside.

Make the dressing: In a small bowl, whisk together the orange juice, shallot, the remaining ½ teaspoon salt, pepper to taste, and the vinegar. Slowly whisk in the olive oil.

Combine the wild rice and jasmine rice in a large bowl. Pour the dressing over and toss. Add the cucumber, bell pepper, currants or cranberries, parsley, and capers and toss together well. You can make this up to 1 day ahead of time and keep covered in the fridge, but don't add the cucumbers until just before serving.

Sprinkle in the nuts just before serving, so they stay crunchy.

CARNITAS

Carnitas (literally, "little meats" in Spanish) might be your favorite filler for a taco, but it's about to become your greatest buffet hit. We're talking about pork that's braised until it falls apart. Serve the tender, flavorful meat with tortillas or rice and beans to soak up all the delicious juices, and add a side of Tomatillo Salsa (recipe follows).

4- TO 5-POUND PORK BUTT (BOSTON BUTT), CUT INTO 5-INCH CHUNKS

COARSE SALT

GRATED ZEST OF 1 ORANGE

1 YELLOW ONION, CHOPPED

3 TO 5 GARLIC CLOVES, CHOPPED

1 TEASPOON GROUND CUMIN (PREFERABLY TOASTED AND GROUND CUMIN SEEDS)

1 TEASPOON DRIED OREGANO

2 SMALL BAY LEAVES

1 CINNAMON STICK

½ TEASPOON PEPPERCORNS

4 CUPS CHICKEN STOCK

Preheat the oven to 350°F.

Season the meat liberally with salt. In a large heavy-bottomed ovenproof pot, combine the meat with the orange zest, onion, garlic, cumin, oregano, bay leaves, cinnamon stick, and peppercorns. Add the chicken stock and enough cold water to just cover the meat.

Place the pot in the oven and braise, uncovered, until the pork begins to fall apart, about 2½ hours. Remove the pork from the liquid and set aside until cool enough to handle. Discard the cooking liquid or strain it and save it for another use, such as braising vegetables. Discard the bay leaves, cinnamon stick, and peppercorns. Turn the oven up to 400°F.

continued

Shred the pork with your hands, removing any large bits of fat, and put it back in the pot. Return the pot to the oven and cook the meat, stirring frequently, for about 20 minutes, or until nicely browned and crispy. This dish can be made ahead and reheated before serving.

Tomatillo Salsa

MAKES ABOUT 3 CUPS

This green hot sauce, or salsa verde, is a staple of Mexican cuisine, served alongside tacos or quesadillas and splashed onto meat and fish dishes. It goes perfectly with the Carnitas.

1½ POUNDS TOMATILLOS (ABOUT 12), HUSKED, RINSED, AND CORED

½ CUP CHOPPED ONION

1 GARLIC CLOVE, COARSELY CHOPPED

1 TABLESPOON FRESHLY SQUEEZED LIME JUICE

1 JALAPEÑO, CORED, SEEDED, AND COARSELY CHOPPED

COARSE SALT

EXTRA-VIRGIN OLIVE OIL

½ CUP FRESH CILANTRO LEAVES

Preheat the broiler.

Put the tomatillos on a rimmed baking sheet and broil, turning them over once, until lightly charred, about 6 minutes. Let cool.

In a blender, combine the tomatillos, onion, garlic, lime juice, jalapeño, salt to taste, and a splash of extra-virgin olive oil.

Pulse until all the ingredients are combined, but some texture remains. Pulse in the cilantro leaves.

MAC 'N' CHEESE

SERVES 10 TO 12 AS A BUFFET DISH OR 5 OR 6 AS AN ENTRÉE

Everyone loves mac 'n' cheese. Here's a foolproof recipe that you can use as a base, adding meat or vegetables if you want more of a one-pot meal.

3 TABLESPOONS UNSALTED BUTTER

1 CUP PANKO
(JAPANESE BREAD CRUMBS)

COARSE SALT

1 POUND PENNE RIGATE
(CAVATAPPI WORKS WELL, TOO)

BÉCHAMEL SAUCE (RECIPE FOLLOWS)

8 OUNCES SHARP CHEDDAR, GRATED

8 OUNCES GRUYÈRE, GRATED

¾ CUP FRESHLY GRATED
PARMIGIANO-REGGIANO

Preheat the oven to 375°F. Bring a big pot of water to a boil.

Meanwhile, melt the butter. Brush a 2-quart casserole dish with 1 tablespoon of the melted butter. In a medium bowl, combine the panko and the remaining 2 tablespoons melted butter, stirring to mix. Set aside.

Add a few big pinches of salt to the boiling water, and then add the pasta. Cook for about 9 minutes, or until the pasta is just shy of al dente. Drain and set aside in a big bowl.

Meanwhile, make the Béchamel Sauce. Once it's cooked, turn off the heat and stir in the Cheddar, Gruyère, and ½ cup of the Parmigiano-Reggiano. Pour the cheese sauce over the pasta and mix well. Add any other ingredients you choose (see opposite). It may seem very saucy, but it will thicken when you bake it and the pasta absorbs the sauce.

Transfer to the prepared baking dish and sprinkle the top with the buttered panko and the remaining ¼ cup Parmigiano-Reggiano. (You can let the dish cool to room temperature, cover it with plastic wrap, and refrigerate for 1 to 2 days or until you're ready to bake.)

Bake for 30 minutes, or until the top is golden and the sauce is bubbling. (If you refrigerated it, it will take about an hour to heat.) Let cool for about 10 minutes before serving.

MAC 'N' CHEESE ADD-INS

....

1 cup diced cooked ham, 2 ounces chopped prosciutto, 1½ cups blanched broccoli florets, 1 to 2 cups sautéed mushrooms, or chopped fresh herbs, such as thyme or rosemary.

Béchamel Sauce

MAKES 4 CUPS

Béchamel (*besciamella* in Italian) is a white sauce in French and Italian cooking, used in many lasagna dishes and as the base for lots of other sauces. Perhaps because it's French, people think it's very tricky, but the only trick is to stir it constantly so it doesn't get lumpy.

4 TABLESPOONS UNSALTED BUTTER, PLUS A SMALL PIECE FOR STORING THE SAUCE

1 SMALL ONION, CHOPPED

1 GARLIC CLOVE, MINCED

4 CUPS MILK

¼ CUP ALL-PURPOSE FLOUR

1 TEASPOON COARSE SALT

CAYENNE PEPPER

FRESHLY GROUND BLACK PEPPER

FRESHLY GRATED NUTMEG

Melt the butter in a saucepan over medium heat. Add the onion and garlic and sauté until translucent, 6 to 8 minutes.

continued

Meanwhile, in a separate pot, heat 2 cups of the milk just to warm it.

Add the flour to the butter mixture and cook, stirring constantly, for about 3 minutes, or until the flour has absorbed the butter and the mixture has begun to thicken.

Slowly pour in the warm milk, stirring constantly to prevent lumps from forming. Once the warm milk has been incorporated, stir in the remaining 2 cups milk and turn the heat up to medium-high. Add the salt, a dash of cayenne, a dash of black pepper, and a dash of nutmeg and cook, stirring constantly, until the sauce thickens, 8 to 10 minutes.

Bring to a boil, then reduce the heat to a bare simmer and cook for 10 minutes longer, stirring constantly to avoid scorching. If not using right away, transfer to a bowl or other container and rub the piece of butter over the top to prevent a skin from forming; refrigerate, covered, after the sauce has cooled off a bit.

BAKED ORECCHIETTE WITH SAUSAGE AND BROCCOLI RABE

SERVES 10 TO 12 AS A BUFFET DISH OR 6 AS AN ENTRÉE

Broccoli rabe and sausage is a classic pairing, and here it's joined by tomatoes, cheese, and cream in a baked pasta dish that is as comforting as it is complex. This is great for a buffet, and also as a meal unto itself. The spicy sausage and bitter greens make this a dish for grown-ups.

UNSALTED BUTTER, FOR THE CASSEROLE DISH

1 POUND HOT ITALIAN SAUSAGES, CASINGS REMOVED

1 TABLESPOON EXTRA-VIRGIN OLIVE OIL

RED PEPPER FLAKES

2 GARLIC CLOVES, SLICED

1 BUNCH OF BROCCOLI RABE, THICK STEMS REMOVED, CHOPPED

COARSE SALT

1 PINT GRAPE OR CHERRY TOMATOES

1 CUP POMÌ BRAND STRAINED TOMATOES OR TOMATO SAUCE

1½ CUPS HEAVY CREAM

1 POUND ORECCHIETTE

8 OUNCES FONTINA, CUT INTO ¼-INCH CUBES

1 CUP GRATED PECORINO

Preheat the oven to 400°F. Butter a 3-quart casserole dish. Bring a large pot of water to a boil.

Meanwhile, place the sausage meat in a cold sauté pan, breaking it up with a wooden spoon. Turn the heat to medium-high and cook the sausage until it begins to brown, about 7 minutes. Remove to paper towels to drain.

continued

Pour off the excess fat in the pan, add the olive oil, a pinch of red pepper flakes, and the garlic, and cook over medium heat until the garlic is golden, 4 to 5 minutes. Add the broccoli rabe, sprinkle with salt, toss, cover, and cook for 1 to 2 minutes, until the greens wilt. Add the cherry tomatoes and cook until they burst, 5 to 7 minutes. Add the strained tomatoes or tomato sauce and the heavy cream and bring to a simmer. Add the sausage and stir well.

Meanwhile, when the water comes to a boil, add a few big pinches of salt and the orecchiette and cook for about 9 minutes, or until the pasta is just shy of al dente. Drain the pasta.

Toss the pasta with the tomato-cream sauce, Fontina, and ½ cup of the Pecorino. Pour the mixture into the prepared baking dish. Sprinkle the remaining ½ cup Pecorino on top, and bake for 20 to 25 minutes, or until golden and bubbling.

LASAGNA WITH RICOTTA AND MUSHROOMS

SERVES 12 TO 14 AS A BUFFET DISH OR 6 TO 8 AS AN ENTRÉE

This creamy, meaty lasagna can be served as a one-dish meal with just a salad, or it can be the star of a buffet. It can be assembled ahead of time and left in the fridge until party time, and it holds up beautifully during a casual party where your friends help themselves (and they will come back for seconds). Béchamel Sauce (page 61) can replace the layers of ricotta if you prefer a more classic, slightly richer lasagna.

3 TABLESPOONS OLIVE OIL

3 ONIONS, 1 MINCED AND 2 SLICED

3 GARLIC CLOVES, SLICED

RED PEPPER FLAKES

1 CELERY RIB, MINCED

1 CARROT, MINCED

1½ POUNDS GROUND BEEF
OR VEAL (OR A COMBINATION)

1 CUP DRY WHITE WINE

1 CUP WHOLE MILK

ONE 6-OUNCE CAN
TOMATO PASTE

ONE 15-OUNCE CAN
CRUSHED TOMATOES

COARSE SALT AND FRESHLY
GROUND BLACK PEPPER

8 OUNCES CREMINI
MUSHROOMS, SLICED

2 HEAPING CUPS WHOLE-MILK
RICOTTA (ABOUT 20 OUNCES)

12 OUNCES MOZZARELLA,
SHREDDED (ABOUT 3 CUPS)

2 LARGE EGGS

⅓ CUP CHOPPED FRESH
FLAT LEAF PARSLEY

1 CUP FRESHLY GRATED
PARMIGIANO-REGGIANO

UNSALTED BUTTER,
FOR THE BAKING DISH

16 SHEETS NO-BOIL
LASAGNA NOODLES

continued

Heat 2 tablespoons of the olive oil in a large saucepan over medium heat and add the minced onion, the garlic, a pinch of red pepper flakes, the celery, and the carrot. Cook until the vegetables have softened, 5 to 7 minutes. Turn the heat to medium-high and add the ground meat. Cook, breaking up the meat, until the liquid has evaporated and the meat begins to brown, about 5 minutes.

Add the wine, milk, tomato paste, crushed tomatoes, 1¾ cups water, and salt and pepper to taste and bring to a boil. Cover, reduce the heat to low, and let the sauce simmer, stirring occasionally, for 45 minutes to 1 hour, until thickened.

Meanwhile, heat the remaining 1 tablespoon olive oil in a large sauté pan over medium-high heat. Add the sliced onions and salt and pepper to taste and cook until the onions are translucent, about 5 minutes. Add the mushrooms and cook until the liquid from the mushrooms evaporates and the mushrooms begin to brown, about 5 minutes. Transfer to a bowl and set aside.

In a large bowl, combine the ricotta, half of the mozzarella, the eggs, the parsley, half of the Parmigiano-Reggiano, and salt and pepper to taste. Stir to combine and set aside.

Preheat the oven to 350°F. Butter a 3-quart baking dish.

Spread 1 cup of the sauce in the bottom of the baking dish. Follow with a layer of no-boil lasagna noodles (about 4 sheets per layer, depending on the size of the dish, overlapping if necessary), 1 cup sauce, and 2 cups of the ricotta mixture. Add another layer of pasta, 1 cup sauce, and half of the mushroom mixture, then a layer of pasta, 1 cup sauce, the remaining ricotta mixture, pasta, and the remaining sauce. Top with the remaining mozzarella and Parmigiano-Reggiano and the remaining mushroom mixture.

Cover the baking dish with greased foil. Put the baking dish on a rimmed baking sheet and bake for 45 minutes. Remove the foil and bake until the top is golden, 15 to 20 minutes more. Let sit for at least 15 minutes before serving.

BAKED CHICKEN WITH APRICOTS AND OLIVES

SERVES 16 AS A BUFFET DISH OR 10 TO 12 AS AN ENTRÉE

With a complex balance of sweet (apricots and honey), salty (olives), and tart (balsamic vinegar and white wine), this is a killer dish. It's a great way to make chicken, that old standby, new and memorable. And because the chicken is cut up, it's a perfect buffet dish: there's no carving to worry about, and your friends can help themselves to their favorite parts.

TWO 3½- TO 4-POUND CHICKENS, PATTED DRY AND CUT INTO 8 PIECES EACH

COARSE SALT AND FRESHLY GROUND BLACK PEPPER

4 TO 6 GARLIC CLOVES, THINLY SLICED

2 TEASPOONS DRIED THYME

¼ CUP BALSAMIC VINEGAR

¼ CUP EXTRA-VIRGIN OLIVE OIL

1 CUP DRIED APRICOTS

½ CUP KALAMATA OLIVES, PITTED

4 BAY LEAVES

½ CUP HONEY

½ CUP DRY WHITE WINE

Season the chicken pieces on all sides with plenty of salt and pepper.

In a large bowl, combine the garlic, thyme, vinegar, olive oil, dried apricots, olives, bay leaves, honey, and wine. Add the chicken to the marinade and turn the pieces over to make sure they're coated.

Cover the bowl or transfer the chicken and marinade to doubled resealable bags and refrigerate for at least 2 hours, or overnight, turning occasionally.

Preheat the oven to 350°F. Line a large roasting pan (or two smaller pans) with aluminum foil.

Arrange the chicken, skin side up, in a single layer in the prepared pan and spoon the marinade, apricots, and olives around and on top of it.

Bake the chicken for 1 hour, basting twice during the second half hour. If the chicken is not golden brown, turn on the broiler and broil for a few minutes to brown the skin.

Transfer the chicken, apricots, and olives to a serving platter and cover lightly with aluminum foil. Discard the bay leaves. Pour the cooking juices through a fine-mesh strainer into a small saucepan, skim off the excess fat, and boil the liquid over medium-high heat until it thickens to a pourable sauce, 5 to 10 minutes.

Pour the sauce over the chicken and serve. This dish is also great at room temperature.

GLAZED HAM

SERVES 20 TO 50 AS A BUFFET DISH OR 12 TO 20 AS AN ENTRÉE

A glazed baked ham is the quintessential buffet dish: traditional and always special. This recipe is foolproof and can be made well ahead of time if you want to serve the ham at room temperature. A tangy, sweet glaze of pomegranate molasses or honey and orange juice provides a perfect foil for the salty cured pork.

A whole, bone-in ham that is brined and then smoked is also known as a "city ham." This is what most people think of when talking about serving a whole cooked ham. You'll find them in your supermarket around the holidays, but if you have a local butcher who smokes his own hams, by all means, buy it there. You can also use a spiral-cut ham and prepare it in the same way, but it won't be as juicy, for obvious reasons. Depending on the weight of the ham you buy, you can feed anywhere from twelve to twenty people for dinner, and many more if it is part of a buffet. If that sounds like a lot, don't worry—the leftovers will feed you for days, or you can send guests home with a care package. And at the very end, you'll have that big ol' bone to make a large pot of soup (see Tip, opposite).

10- TO 15-POUND BONE-IN, FULLY COOKED WHOLE HAM

A HANDFUL OF WHOLE CLOVES (OPTIONAL)

1 CUP LIGHT BROWN SUGAR, PACKED

¾ CUP GRAINY MUSTARD

¼ CUP POMEGRANATE MOLASSES OR HONEY

JUICE OF ½ ORANGE

½ TEASPOON CAYENNE PEPPER

Bring the ham to room temperature; this will take about 2 hours.

Preheat the oven to 350°F.

Line a shallow roasting pan with aluminum foil and place the ham in the pan. Score the ham with the tip of a paring knife, cutting diagonal strips and then crossing them to form 1½-inch diamonds. If desired, stick a whole clove in the center of each diamond.

Bake the ham until the internal temperature reaches 140°F, about 2 hours.

While the ham is in the oven, make the glaze: Combine the brown sugar, mustard, molasses or honey, orange juice, and cayenne in a medium bowl, and whisk until well blended.

Remove the ham from the oven and brush the glaze generously over the surface. Return the ham to the oven for about 1½ hours more, basting every 30 minutes or so, until the glaze is brown and crusty. Remove the ham from the oven and let it rest for 30 minutes before carving.

TIP: SAVE YOUR BONES

Bones—cooked or uncooked, from pork, chicken, beef, or any other meat—shouldn't go in the garbage can until you've rendered all you can from them. If the butcher removes meat from a bone for you, ask to take the bone home so you can make stock from it, or at least give it to the dog as a treat. Nothing could be easier than stock from scratch, and soup is also a great way to use other leftovers from the party, like vegetables from a crudités platter or the meat from a roasted chicken. Bones from a ham, a roasted chicken, or chops of any kind can be collected in the freezer for a rainy day when you have a few hours and a craving for soup.

SIT-DOWN DINNERS

A few foolproof dishes, wine to match, and an easy dessert, and you've mastered the dinner party. The cooking need not be daunting to be impressive. The whole idea is to cook good, simple food and present it in an appetizing way.

Writing a menu may be the most important step in planning your party. Go to the farmers' market or grocery store a week or so in advance of your party and see what looks good. Did you recently clip an intriguing recipe? Is there a theme that will help pull the party together? Find a hook, and then hang everything else on it. Put your ideas on paper, including as much detail as possible, so you can easily spot problems. Usually, the simpler the menu, the more successful the meal.

TRY THIS MENU

GOUGÈRES (PAGE 31)

ROASTED FILET OF BEEF (PAGE 88)

ROASTED FINGERLING POTATOES (PAGE 102)

BIBB SALAD WITH SHALLOT VINAIGRETTE

GLAZED FIGS (SEE PAGE 116)

WHY IT WORKS

Start the evening off on a French note by serving gougères, which is a fancy name for cheese puffs. These can be passed to your guests while they stand and sip an aperitif or wine. Follow with a well-balanced meat-and-potatoes menu that's not too heavy and doesn't repeat the richness of the gougères. The salad, with its bright vinaigrette, will balance the flavors and textures nicely; and a fruit dessert is the perfect finish.

MAIN DISHES

Let's face it: the main dish is the main event at a dinner party, and it's often the dish that takes the most time to prepare. Decide whether you'll be serving meat, poultry, fish or seafood, or a vegetarian dish, and keep the season in mind. A heavy stew in August wouldn't be ideal, nor would a caprese salad in January. Once you've made your selection, choosing complementary side dishes will be a breeze.

TARRAGON ROASTED CHICKEN

SERVES 6 TO 8

There is no better way to show your love than by serving a delicious and fragrant roasted chicken, perfect for almost any occasion. A flavorful rub under the skin and a lovely pan gravy elevate roasted chicken from simple to special.

8 TABLESPOONS (1 STICK) SOFTENED UNSALTED BUTTER

¼ CUP PLUS 1 TABLESPOON CHOPPED FRESH TARRAGON

1 SHALLOT, FINELY MINCED

COARSE SALT AND FRESHLY GROUND BLACK PEPPER

TWO 3½- TO 4-POUND CHICKENS, RINSED AND DRIED, GIBLETS AND EXCESS FAT DISCARDED

1 LEMON, HALVED

2 MEDIUM ONIONS, SLICED INTO ½-INCH-THICK SLICES

¾ CUP WHITE WINE

1 CUP CHICKEN STOCK

1 TABLESPOON DIJON MUSTARD

2 TABLESPOONS HEAVY CREAM (OPTIONAL)

Preheat the oven to 400°F.

Combine 6 tablespoons (¾ stick) of the butter with the ¼ cup tarragon, the shallot, 1½ teaspoons salt, and ½ teaspoon pepper in a small bowl and mix well with a wooden spoon.

Loosen the skin of the breast portion of the chickens by sliding your hands under it, from both ends. Smear the butter mixture all over the breast portion of each chicken, using half of it for each bird. Season the cavities liberally with salt and pepper, and place a lemon half in each one. Tie the legs together, and tuck the wing tips under the body.

continued

Rub the remaining 2 tablespoons butter all over the skin, and season with salt and pepper. The chickens can be prepared to this point up to 1 day in advance and refrigerated.

In a large roasting pan, like the one you would use for a turkey, or two smaller roasting pans, create a "rack" for each chicken by arranging the onion slices close together for each chicken to sit on. If using one large roasting pan, evenly space the onion "racks" so the chickens will have plenty of space around them. Place a chicken on each "rack," their feet pointing in opposite directions.

Place the chickens in the oven to roast. After 20 minutes, reduce the oven temperature to 350°F. Baste the chickens, and continue basting every 15 minutes or so, reversing the pan position each time. Roast until an instant-read thermometer reads 165°F when inserted into the area where the leg meets the body, 1 hour and 15 minutes to 1 hour and 30 minutes. The legs should feel slightly loose, and the juices will run clear.

Transfer the chickens to a platter to rest in a warm spot while you make the sauce. Pour off the fat from the roasting pan, keeping the onions in the pan. Use a paper towel to blot any additional grease from the pan. Place the roasting pan over one or two burners and turn the heat to medium. Pour in the wine and bring to a boil. Scrape up the brown bits from the pan with a wooden spoon. Reduce by half, and add the chicken stock. Bring to a boil, and strain into a small saucepan, pressing down on the solids in the strainer before discarding them.

Whisk in the mustard and heavy cream, if using. Reduce over high heat until slightly thickened, about 10 minutes. Stir in the remaining 1 tablespoon tarragon, and season to taste with salt and pepper.

Carve the chicken into serving pieces and arrange on a warm platter. Serve the sauce on the side.

LAMB TAGINE

Sometimes a slightly exotic dish makes perfect dinner-party fare. Lamb tagine fits the bill, and since it can easily be made a day or two ahead, it's easy on the host, too.

1 TEASPOON GROUND CORIANDER

1 TEASPOON GROUND CUMIN

½ TEASPOON PAPRIKA

1 TEASPOON COARSE SALT

½ TEASPOON FRESHLY GROUND BLACK PEPPER

2 TABLESPOONS OLIVE OIL

3 POUNDS LAMB STEW MEAT, PATTED DRY

2 MEDIUM ONIONS, THINLY SLICED LENGTHWISE

2 CINNAMON STICKS

2 TEASPOONS FRESHLY GRATED PEELED GINGER

CAYENNE PEPPER

1 LARGE GARLIC CLOVE, FINELY GRATED

1 TABLESPOON TOMATO PASTE

1 CUP DRIED APRICOTS

2 TEASPOONS UNSALTED BUTTER

½ CUP COARSELY CHOPPED ALMONDS

COOKED COUSCOUS, FOR SERVING

CHOPPED FRESH FLAT-LEAF PARSLEY, FOR SERVING

Preheat the oven to 325°F.

In a small bowl, combine the coriander, cumin, paprika, salt, and pepper. Stir well and coat the meat with the spice mixture.

Heat a large Dutch oven over medium-high heat and add 1 tablespoon of the olive oil. Add half of the meat, and brown lightly on all sides, 5 to 7 minutes. Transfer to a plate and repeat with the remaining meat, using the remaining 1 tablespoon olive oil.

continued

Return the first batch of meat to the Dutch oven. Add the onions to the pot along with the cinnamon sticks, ginger, a pinch of cayenne, the garlic, and the tomato paste.

Add enough water to almost cover the meat (3 to 4 cups), stir well, and bring to a simmer on top of the stove. Cover with a tight-fitting lid, and transfer to the oven.

Cook for approximately 1½ hours, or until the meat yields to gentle pressure with a fork and feels completely tender. Gently scoop the meat and onions into a large bowl using a slotted spoon. Discard the cinnamon sticks. Degrease the liquid either by skimming it with a ladle or by pouring it into a fat separator and returning the liquid to the pot. Add the apricots to the liquid, and simmer over medium heat until slightly thickened, 10 to 12 minutes.

Return the meat to the pot and coat the meat well with the sauce, heating it thoroughly. If making ahead of time, let cool and refrigerate until close to serving time. Reheat gently in the oven or on the stovetop over medium-low heat.

Heat a small pan over medium-low heat. Add the butter and almonds and cook, stirring frequently, until golden brown. Serve the tagine over cooked couscous with the almonds and parsley over the top.

HOISIN-GLAZED SALMON WITH SOBA NOODLES

SERVES 8

If you know you're serving fish-eaters, salmon is a safe choice, since most people like it. Despite the simplicity of preparation, this dish will impress your guests. Serve with sautéed baby bok choy.

½ CUP HOISIN SAUCE

2 TABLESPOONS FRESHLY SQUEEZED LIME JUICE

1 LARGE GARLIC CLOVE, FINELY GRATED

2 TEASPOONS HONEY

ONE 8-OUNCE PACKAGE SOBA NOODLES

TOASTED SESAME OIL

SOY SAUCE

EIGHT 6- TO 8-OUNCE SKINLESS SALMON FILLETS

COARSE SALT AND FRESHLY GROUND BLACK PEPPER

VEGETABLE OR PEANUT OIL, FOR COATING THE FISH

TOASTED SESAME SEEDS, FOR SPRINKLING

Combine the hoisin sauce, lime juice, garlic, and honey in a small bowl. Blend thoroughly and set aside.

Cook the soba noodles according to package directions. Drain and rinse the noodles. Lightly dress with toasted sesame oil and soy sauce. Set aside.

Preheat the oven to 425°F. Line a rimmed baking sheet with aluminum foil or parchment paper.

Season the salmon fillets with salt and pepper and lightly coat with vegetable oil. Heat a large nonstick sauté pan over medium-high heat and arrange 4 of the salmon fillets in the pan. Sauté until golden, 2 to 3 minutes on each side. Transfer to the prepared baking sheet and repeat with the remaining salmon.

Brush the hoisin glaze evenly over the salmon fillets. The salmon can be prepared ahead to this point. Store in the refrigerator until shortly before ready to cook.

Place the salmon in the oven and cook for 10 to 12 minutes, or until the desired doneness is reached, basting with the glaze several times.

Serve with the room-temperature soba noodles and sautéed baby bok choy. Sprinkle toasted sesame seeds over the top.

PORK TENDERLOIN WITH POMEGRANATE SAUCE

SERVES 8

Pork tenderloin is an inexpensive cut of meat that is available everywhere, is easy and fast to cook, and dresses up nicely with ruby-red sauce made from pomegranate juice and demi-glace. Store-bought demi-glace or glace de viande is the best way to approximate the flavor of a restaurant sauce at home. It can be found in fancy food stores either as a thick concentrate or frozen. If you want to make this dish partially ahead of time, sear the meat as directed in the second step, then deglaze the pan and complete the sauce. Bring the meat back to room temperature for about 30 minutes before roasting and serving. Potato Gratin (page 101) and blanched haricots verts (see page 106) would make delicious side dishes.

4 PORK TENDERLOINS (ABOUT 1 POUND EACH), EXCESS FAT AND SILVERSKIN TRIMMED

COARSE SALT AND FRESHLY GROUND BLACK PEPPER

2 CUPS POMEGRANATE JUICE

2 TABLESPOONS OLIVE OIL

½ CUP DRY RED WINE

1 SHALLOT, MINCED

1 CUP DEMI-GLACE (1 TABLESPOON RECONSTITUTED WITH 1 CUP WATER OR 1 CUP THINNED)

1 FRESH THYME SPRIG

1 TO 2 TABLESPOONS COLD UNSALTED BUTTER

POMEGRANATE SEEDS, FOR SERVING

continued

Preheat the oven to 375°F.

Tie the tenderloins with butcher's twine, to hold their round shape during cooking. Season with salt and pepper.

Bring the pomegranate juice to a simmer in a small saucepan over medium heat, and simmer until it is reduced to a syrupy consistency, about 20 minutes. Set the pan aside.

Heat a large ovenproof skillet, preferably cast iron, over medium-high heat. Add 1 tablespoon of the olive oil and heat until hot. Place 2 of the tenderloins in the pan and sear well on all sides, about 10 minutes. Transfer to a rimmed baking sheet. Repeat with the remaining tenderloins, using the remaining 1 tablespoon olive oil. Transfer to the baking sheet.

Roast the meat in the oven until the internal temperature reaches 130°F, about 20 minutes. Transfer to a plate and loosely tent with foil.

While the meat is resting, finish the sauce: Add the wine and shallot to the skillet, bring to a simmer over high heat, stirring with a wooden spoon to loosen the brown bits, and simmer until the wine is reduced by half, about 5 minutes. Add the demi-glace and thyme and reduce until the mixture is thick and syrupy, about 8 minutes. Strain the sauce through a fine-mesh sieve into the pomegranate syrup. Season to taste with salt and pepper and bring to a boil. Remove from the heat and stir in enough of the cold butter to give the sauce body.

Slice the pork into 2-inch lengths. Stand 3 pieces of pork on end, closely touching, on each of 8 warm plates. Pour a bit of sauce over the meat, and top with a few pomegranate seeds. Serve immediately.

BRAISED SHORT RIBS

SERVES 4 TO 6

Short ribs are extraordinarily rich, so serve what might seem like a smallish portion, and with the exception of creamy mashed potatoes, keep the rest of the menu on the light side. A raw kale salad or a cold green bean salad will help cut the richness of the meat. Make sure to buy the right kind of short ribs for this recipe—the choices can be confusing. Short ribs that are cut parallel to the bone are known as English-style or English-cut short ribs. When the short ribs are cut across the bone, they are known as flanken-style.

3 POUNDS ENGLISH-CUT SHORT RIBS

1 TABLESPOON FRESH THYME LEAVES, PLUS TWO SPRIGS

PEEL OF 1 ORANGE, SLICED

6 GARLIC CLOVES, SMASHED

2 TEASPOONS FRESHLY GROUND BLACK PEPPER

COARSE SALT

2 TABLESPOONS EXTRA-VIRGIN OLIVE OIL

2 MEDIUM CARROTS, DICED

1 ONION, DICED

2 CELERY RIBS, DICED

2 BAY LEAVES

ONE 750-ML BOTTLE DRY RED WINE

2 TABLESPOONS BALSAMIC VINEGAR

6 CUPS LOW-SODIUM VEAL OR BEEF STOCK

Rub the short ribs with the thyme leaves, orange peel, garlic, and pepper. Put the meat in a resealable plastic bag and refrigerate overnight.

The next day, remove the ribs from the fridge about 30 minutes before cooking to allow them to come to room temperature.

Discard the orange peel and garlic. Season the ribs well with salt on all sides. Heat a large skillet over high

heat. Add the olive oil and heat until hot. Sear the ribs until dark brown and crusty on all sides, using tongs to turn. Remove the meat to a heavy-bottomed braising pot with a lid (enameled cast iron is ideal).

Pour off most of the fat from the skillet and add the carrots, onion, celery, bay leaves, and thyme sprigs.

Preheat the oven to 325°F.

Reduce the heat under the skillet to medium and sauté the vegetables, stirring occasionally, until tender, 6 to 8 minutes. Add the wine and vinegar, turn the heat up, and simmer until the liquid reduces by half.

Add the veal or beef stock and bring to a boil. Pour the mixture over the ribs in the braising pot. They should be nearly submerged in the liquid.

Cover the pot, put it into the oven, and braise the short ribs for about 3 hours, until the meat is very tender. With a slotted spoon, transfer the ribs to a platter and remove the bones. Strain the cooking liquid and skim the excess fat from the top; discard the vegetables. Pour the liquid into a saucepan, bring to a boil, and boil to thicken it slightly. Pour the sauce over the meat and reheat if necessary.

NOTE
To store leftovers, add the meat directly to the sauce, cover, and refrigerate for up to 3 days.

ROASTED FILET OF BEEF

SERVES 8

As long as you have a carnivorous crowd, it's hard to go wrong serving a whole beef tenderloin. It's expensive, yes, but it's also incredibly easy and fast to cook. Serve with simple roasted carrots (see page 104) for a classic pairing that always pleases.

ONE 3-POUND FILET OF BEEF

OLIVE OIL

COARSE SALT AND FRESHLY GROUND BLACK PEPPER

2 SHALLOTS, MINCED

1 FRESH THYME SPRIG

1 TABLESPOON UNSALTED BUTTER

½ CUP DRY RED WINE

½ CUP HEAVY CREAM

Preheat the oven to 375°F.

Rub the beef with olive oil. Season on all sides with salt and pepper.

Heat a large ovenproof skillet over high heat and sear the meat until well browned, about 10 minutes.

Transfer the skillet to the oven and roast the meat for 15 to 20 minutes, or until the internal temperature reaches 130°F. Transfer to a cutting board, cover with aluminum foil, and let rest for 10 minutes.

Meanwhile, sweat the shallots and thyme sprig in the butter in a small saucepan over low heat until the shallots are translucent and tender. Add the wine and simmer until reduced by half. Strain through a fine-mesh sieve and return the sauce to the saucepan. Add the heavy cream and simmer until reduced to a velvety sauce.

Slice the meat and serve with the sauce drizzled over it.

ROASTED TURKEY PARTS

Order in advance, so your butcher can cut the turkey into quarters for you.

ONE 12-POUND FRESH TURKEY, CUT INTO 2 BREASTS AND 2 LEGS

COARSE SALT AND FRESHLY GROUND BLACK PEPPER

2 FRESH ROSEMARY SPRIGS, CHOPPED

OLIVE OIL

2 CARROTS, CUT INTO CHUNKS

2 CELERY RIBS, CUT INTO CHUNKS

2 ONIONS, CUT INTO QUARTERS

Preheat the oven to 400°F.

Season the turkey breasts and legs with salt and pepper and the rosemary and drizzle with olive oil.

Place the turkey legs in a large roasting pan. Add the carrots, celery, and onions.

Roast the legs for 10 minutes. Add the breasts to the pan and continue roasting for 1 hour, basting occasionally with the pan drippings; add water to the pan if necessary to keep the drippings from scorching. Check the internal temperatures of the turkey parts with an instant-read thermometer: the legs should reach 180°F, the breasts 165°F in the thickest part.

ROASTED TURKEY

SERVES 8 TO 10

One thing that will ease your way to cooking a delicious bird is a good roasting pan; even if you use it just once a year, it is worth the investment.

ONE 10- TO 12-POUND FRESH TURKEY, PATTED DRY INSIDE AND OUT, GIBLETS AND NECK RESERVED

12 TABLESPOONS (1½ STICKS) UNSALTED BUTTER, 4 TABLESPOONS SOFTENED

COARSE SALT AND FRESHLY GROUND BLACK PEPPER

3 TABLESPOONS CHOPPED FRESH ROSEMARY

1 HEAD OF GARLIC (UNPEELED)

1 HANDFUL OF FRESH THYME SPRIGS

1¾ CUPS DRY WHITE WINE

Preheat the oven to 375°F.

Rub the turkey with the softened butter. Season inside and out with salt and pepper and the rosemary. Stuff the garlic and thyme sprigs into the cavity. Place the turkey on a rack in a roasting pan.

In a saucepan, melt the rest of the butter with 1 cup of the wine. Cut a piece of cheesecloth to cover the breast in 4 layers, about 16 inches, and soak it in the butter-wine mixture. Fold the cheesecloth into quarters and drape over the turkey breast.

Pour the remaining wine and ¾ cup water into the roasting pan, place in the oven, and roast for 2 hours. Baste the turkey every half hour with the liquid in the pan. Add more water if the pan is dry. Keep the cheesecloth moist.

Remove the cheesecloth after 2 hours and continue cooking the turkey for 1 more hour until an instant-read thermometer inserted in the thickest part of a thigh reads 180°F and of the breast reads 165°F. Let the bird rest before carving.

FISH EN PAPILLOTE

SERVES 4

Use this recipe as a guide, but you can also add other ingredients that will flavor the fish. Try a few capers, sliced ginger, chopped scallions, thyme sprigs, a drop of sesame oil, some sliced oil-cured olives, or even a few chopped tomatoes.

2 CUPS THINLY SLICED FENNEL, PLUS SOME OF THE FRONDS

1 LARGE SHALLOT, THINLY SLICED

4 THICK SKINLESS FISH FILLETS, ABOUT 6 OUNCES EACH, SUCH AS STRIPED BASS, HALIBUT, OR SNAPPER

COARSE SALT AND FRESHLY GROUND BLACK PEPPER

1 CUP SLICED SHIITAKE MUSHROOMS

4 TEASPOONS UNSALTED BUTTER (OPTIONAL)

OLIVE OIL (OPTIONAL)

Preheat the oven to 400°F.

Measure four 24-inch-long sheets of parchment. Fold each sheet in half and, starting from the folded side, cut a large half-heart shape.

Open one heart on a work surface. Place one-quarter of the sliced fennel a few inches from the center crease of the heart. Scatter one-quarter of the shallots over it. Place a fish fillet on top, parallel to the crease, and season with salt and pepper. Scatter one-quarter of the mushrooms and some fennel fronds over the top, and, if desired, top with the butter or a drizzle of olive oil in the center.

Fold the paper over to enclose the fish and vegetables, and begin folding the edges over: Make short folds, beginning at the deep center of the heart and working your way to the point of the heart. Each fold should overlap the previous fold; the folds will get gradually longer as you work your way around. After you fold the last pleat under, use a metal paper clip to secure it; you can also place a paper clip on the first fold to ensure a tight seal.

Refrigerate the packet and repeat with the remaining ingredients.

Place the packets on rimmed baking sheets and bake for 15 to 18 minutes, or until the packages are puffy.

SIDES

Sides can be incredibly simple and straightforward and still complement the star player perfectly. Aim to provide contrasting flavors and
textures, and color as well. Think of something cooling to counter
something hot (fluffy jasmine rice with a spicy shrimp stir-fry), or
something crunchy alongside something comfortingly soft (a green
bean vinaigrette with a braised brisket). Also, for your own sake, plan
to make only one labor-intensive dish (if any!), and balance that one
with easy side-dish preparations to play the supporting role.

THE ART OF THE SALAD

Starting your guests off with an appetite-whetting salad, or serving it as one of the side dishes, is a fairly standard approach to the dinner party, and it's also an easy, elegant way to show off your inner chef—no cooking required! Here are some surefire hits. The dressing suggestions, in black, should be mixed at a ratio of 3 parts oil to 1 part acid, or closer to 2 to 1 if you like your dressing more acidic.

1. SHAVED FENNEL, BABY ARUGULA, GRAPEFRUIT AND/ OR ORANGE SEGMENTS, AND PITTED KALAMATA OLIVES. Citrus juice, extra-virgin olive oil, salt, and pepper.

2. CHOPPED ESCAROLE, THINLY SLICED RADISHES, AND TOASTED RYE CROUTONS. Dijon mustard, garlic, anchovy paste, freshly squeezed lemon juice, extra-virgin olive oil, salt, and pepper.

3. SHAVED CARROTS AND CUCUMBERS, PEA SHOOTS, AND DILL SPRIGS. Drizzle of vinegar, extra-virgin olive oil, salt, and pepper.

4. SLICED HEIRLOOM TOMATOES, TORN LETTUCE, SHREDDED BASIL LEAVES, AND SLICED GOAT CHEESE. Drizzle of extra-virgin olive oil, salt, and pepper.

5. THINLY SLICED CELERY, CELERY LEAVES, SLICED PICKLED OR COOKED BEETS, THINLY SLICED PEAR, CHOPPED WALNUTS, AND THINLY SLICED BLUE CHEESE. Drizzle of extra-virgin olive oil, freshly squeezed lemon juice, salt, and pepper.

6. SHREDDED BRUSSELS SPROUTS AND COOKED CRUMBLED BACON. Plain yogurt drink, red wine vinegar, chopped chives, salt, pepper, and extra-virgin olive oil.

CLASSIC POTATO DISHES

If you're not sure what to pair with your main course, chances are one of these will be perfect. Think about what will best complement what you are serving. Use mashed potatoes when there's a delicious, meaty sauce to catch. Pair the creamy gratin with something not too rich. Roasted potatoes are a crowd-pleaser, and they go with almost anything; you can even serve them as an hors d'oeuvre accompanied by a spicy mayonnaise dip.

Mashed Potatoes

1¾ POUNDS YUKON GOLD POTATOES, CUT IN HALF

1¾ TEASPOONS COARSE SALT (OR TO TASTE)

1 CUP MILK

2 TABLESPOONS UNSALTED BUTTER

¼ TEASPOON FRESHLY GROUND BLACK PEPPER

Place the potatoes in a medium saucepan, add water to cover by 1 inch and 1 teaspoon of the salt, and bring to a boil over high heat. Reduce to a simmer and cook until the potatoes are easily pierced with a knife, about 20 minutes. Drain.

As soon as the potatoes are cool enough to handle, peel them. Push the potatoes through a ricer or food mill back into the saucepan, or mash with a masher in the pan.

Heat the milk in a small saucepan or in the microwave. Add the butter, the remaining ¾ teaspoon salt, and the pepper to the potatoes, then add as much of the milk as needed to create the desired consistency, stirring until well combined. Taste for seasoning, and serve hot.

Potato Gratin

SERVES 6

UNSALTED BUTTER

1½ CUPS HEAVY CREAM

1 FRESH THYME SPRIG

2 GARLIC CLOVES

2 POUNDS RUSSET (BAKING) POTATOES, THINLY SLICED

COARSE SALT AND FRESHLY GROUND BLACK PEPPER

¼ CUP FRESHLY GRATED PARMIGIANO-REGGIANO

Preheat the oven to 375°F. Butter a 2-quart gratin dish or 6 individual baking dishes.

Combine the heavy cream, thyme, and garlic in a small saucepan and bring to just under a boil. Remove from the heat. Spread one-third of the potatoes evenly in the gratin dish or individual baking dishes. Dot the potatoes with butter, season with salt and pepper, and sprinkle with the Parmigiano-Reggiano.

Repeat twice, to make 3 layers of potatoes. Pour the warm cream over the potatoes.

Bake until bubbling and brown, 35 to 45 minutes (less time for the individual dishes).

Roasted Fingerling Potatoes

SERVES 4

1½ POUNDS FINGERLING POTATOES, WASHED AND DRIED

1 TABLESPOON OLIVE OIL

½ TEASPOON COARSE SALT

¼ TEASPOON FRESHLY GROUND BLACK PEPPER

1 TABLESPOON CHOPPED FRESH ROSEMARY

4 OR 5 UNPEELED GARLIC CLOVES

Preheat the oven to 425°F.

Halve larger potatoes and leave small ones whole, so they are uniform in size.

In a large bowl, toss the potatoes with the olive oil, salt, pepper, rosemary, and garlic.

Spray a large rimmed baking sheet with cooking spray or coat it with olive oil. Spread the potatoes on the baking sheet, cut side down, and roast until tender and golden brown, about 20 minutes.

ROASTED VEGETABLES

Starchy or fibrous vegetables are best for roasting. Because by nature they are drier than leafy vegetables, root vegetables are successfully cooked with dry heat, rather than steamed or boiled. Sautéing is tricky because they are so dense and require a long cooking time. In the oven, they can achieve the perfect balance of browned, even crisp, outsides and soft, creamy insides. Roasting is a very simple way to make very satisfying, beautiful side dishes. Be sure to turn the vegetables toward the end; they will be golden on all sides.

Preheat the oven to 425°F. Toss the vegetables with olive oil, salt, and pepper. A rimmed baking sheet (nonstick is a plus) is ideal for most roasting, but you can use a roasting pan or a cast-iron skillet. Large vegetables will cook much faster and have more caramelized surface area per bite if they are cut into smaller pieces, but be mindful to cut the pieces to a uniform size so they cook evenly. And don't crowd the pan, or you will create steam and end up with less brown and more mush. This is essential: there should be just one layer of vegetables with some space around each piece. The cut vegetables should be placed cut side down to start so they get nice and brown.

BABY EGGPLANT

To roast, cut small eggplant lengthwise in half, large ones into chunks. Cook for 13 to 15 minutes, cut side down, or until brown and tender. *Cook with* garlic. *Finish with* mint or parsley and tahini, or with Sriracha, sesame seeds, and sesame oil. *Serve with* Asian-style grilled marinated beef or lamb, or in a tomato sauce with pasta.

BRUSSELS SPROUTS

To roast, cut in half if large. Cook for 20 to 25 minutes, turning after 15 minutes. *Cook with* shallots. *Finish with* walnut oil, toasted walnuts or pine nuts, and crisp crumbled bacon. *Serve with* turkey or chicken.

CAULIFLOWER

To roast, cut into bite-size pieces. Cook for 20 to 25 minutes, gently stirring or flipping after 10 minutes. *Cook with* unpeeled garlic cloves. *Finish with* raisins, capers, bread crumbs, and freshly grated Parmigiano-Reggiano. *Serve with* pot roast, veal chops, or steak.

CELERIAC AND TURNIPS

To roast, cut into wedges. Cook for 30 minutes, turning after 20 minutes. *Cook with* garlic, thyme, and sliced onions. *Finish with* parsley. *Serve with* braised meat or chicken.

PARSNIPS AND CARROTS

To roast, peel and cut lengthwise in half. Cook for 30 minutes, gently stirring or turning after 20 minutes. *Cook with* fresh thyme sprigs. *Finish with* nutmeg. *Serve with* braised or roasted beef or lamb, or roasted chicken.

BLANCHED VEGETABLES

Blanching, which is boiling vegetables very briefly in salted water, is an important technique. Blanching is generally useful for hardy, fibrous vegetables that would take a long time to sauté from raw or that you want to leave crisp. Blanching brings out the vibrant green of broccoli or string beans but leaves them firm and crisp enough to go into a sauté pan, where they will get more flavor, or into a salad, to be simply dressed with a vinaigrette.

The keys to successful blanching are to salt the water generously and to have an ice bath ready to "shock" the veggies. Fill a bowl with ice and cold water and leave it in the sink, waiting while you blanch. When the veggies are done, drain them and submerge them quickly in the ice water. This will stop them from cooking (or overcooking) and ensure that the bright green color doesn't fade to gray. Keep in mind that you'll want some time to dry the vegetables before throwing them into a salad or a hot skillet. But blanching and shocking can be done ahead of time, so the clever host has to worry only about the finishing flavors at the last minute.

ASPARAGUS

To blanch, snap off the tough bottoms and boil the spears for 1 to 3 minutes, depending on thickness. Shock in an ice bath. *Finish with* lemon juice and/or grated zest, chopped almonds, butter, parsley, or truffle oil. *Serve with* lamb or grilled fish or in salads or risotto.

BROCCOLI RABE

To blanch, trim the thickest stems and boil for 2 to 3 minutes; shock in an ice bath. *Sauté with* garlic, olive oil, red pepper flakes, and caramelized onions. *Serve with* sausages, or in pasta with ricotta and Parmigiano-Reggiano.

BROCCOLI FLORETS

To blanch, boil for 1 to 2 minutes; shock in an ice bath. *Finish with* ground cumin, garlic, red pepper flakes, soy sauce, or sesame seeds. *Serve in* salads or pasta dishes, or on crudités platters.

HARICOTS VERTS OR GREEN BEANS

To blanch, boil haricots verts (thin French beans) for 1 minute, and thick string beans for 2 minutes. Shock in an ice bath. *Finish with* caramelized shallots, sautéed garlic, vinaigrette, lemon and olive oil, parsley, crumbled blue cheese, chopped walnuts, walnut oil, or pesto. *Serve with* salmon, roasted meat or chicken, or boiled potatoes, or in pasta salads.

SAUTÉED VEGETABLES

To sauté means to cook in a skillet with some fat. Most often, you sauté veggies that don't require an extended cooking time. Many vegetables will wilt, creating a bit of steam as they break down. Anything you sauté will pick up the flavor of whatever it's cooked with, such as the oil or butter you're using and any garlic, onions, or herbs you throw in the skillet.

The trick to sautéing is regulating the heat. A very hot skillet can get some color on your vegetables, which you may want in some cases—for example, if you're cooking small peppers that you want to stay crisp but become brown in some spots. Generally, though, your flame should be somewhere in the medium range. A very hot pan can burn your food before it cooks through, turn butter into a smoky disaster, or send grease flying dangerously. If the heat is too low, your vegetables may absorb a lot of fat without getting cooked. Taste things as you go, and stay involved, trusting your judgment to adjust the flame as needed.

Leafy greens such as spinach, kale, and chard will cook down to a fraction of their original volume. This means you should always make more than what looks like enough, and keep in mind that your seasonings will be concentrated: a giant pinch of salt may look like the right amount when you begin but will result in overly salty greens.

MUSHROOMS

Depending on the type and size, slice them or quarter them. *Cook with* shallots or garlic, thyme or rosemary. *Finish with* tarragon, parsley, or chives. *Serve with* steak, mashed potatoes, chicken, or fettuccine with Parmigiano-Reggiano.

SNOW PEAS

Snip off the stem end. *Cook with* garlic, scallions, shallots, or sliced ginger. *Finish with* sesame oil, sesame seeds, grated lemon zest, and soy sauce. *Serve with* grilled fish, or chicken paillards.

SWISS CHARD

Separate the leaves from the stems, chop the stems into 1-inch pieces, and roughly chop the leaves. Cook the stems a few minutes longer than the leaves. *Cook with* garlic and onions. *Finish with* crisp pancetta, freshly squeezed lemon juice, and red pepper flakes. *Serve with* pasta, roasted meat, fish—anything you would serve spinach with.

YELLOW SQUASH AND ZUCCHINI

Slice into ¼-inch-thick half-moons. *Cook with* cherry tomatoes and basil or thyme. *Finish with* Parmigiano-Reggiano and toasted sliced almonds. *Serve with* grilled meat, chicken, fish, eggs, or pasta.

6

DESSERTS

You should offer your guests something sweet at the end of a great meal. The dessert shouldn't be overwhelming on the guests' palate or overly complicated and time-consuming for the host. Simple assembled desserts that involve simple ingredients are great for a sit-down dinner, but you can also attempt something slightly more involved like a pie or a soufflé. In most cases you will be able to get that out of the way the night before or first thing the morning of the party. Here are some great ideas and fail-safe recipes to inspire the end of your meal.

MIXED BERRY CRISP

A warm berry crisp is sure to win over your guests with its irresistibly comforting flavor and rich aroma, and it is one of the easiest desserts to prepare. The topping can be made any time and stored in the freezer in a resealable plastic bag. This recipe is designed to be quick to prepare; there is absolutely no prep work for the fruit aside from washing the berries!

TOPPING

1 CUP PLUS 2 TABLESPOONS ALL-PURPOSE FLOUR (IF YOU ARE PREPARING INDIVIDUAL RAMEKINS, REDUCE THE FLOUR TO 1 CUP)

⅓ CUP DARK OR LIGHT BROWN SUGAR, PACKED

½ CUP GRANULATED SUGAR

¼ TEASPOON GROUND CINNAMON

¼ TEASPOON BAKING POWDER

¼ TEASPOON SALT

8 TABLESPOONS (1 STICK) CHILLED UNSALTED BUTTER, CUT INTO PIECES

FILLING

UNSALTED BUTTER, FOR THE BAKING DISH

6 CUPS MIXED BERRIES (RASPBERRIES, BLUEBERRIES, AND BLACKBERRIES)

½ CUP GRANULATED SUGAR

3 TABLESPOONS ALL-PURPOSE FLOUR

1 TEASPOON GRATED LEMON ZEST

JUICE OF ½ LEMON

To make the topping, combine the flour, brown sugar, granulated sugar, cinnamon, baking powder, and salt in a food processor and pulse to mix evenly. Add the butter and pulse until the mixture comes together and clumps. Chill in the refrigerator for 30 minutes.

Preheat the oven to 375°F. Butter a 2-quart baking dish or 6 to 8 individual ramekins placed on a rimmed baking sheet.

continued

To make the filling, in a large bowl, combine the berries, granulated sugar, flour, lemon zest, and lemon juice.

Transfer the filling to the baking dish or divide it among the ramekins. Spoon the topping evenly over the filling. Bake for 35 to 45 minutes, for a large crisp, or about 25 minutes for individual crisps, until the topping is golden brown and the juices are thick and bubbling.

MALTED BROWNIES

Kids will go crazy for these, of course, but so will grown-ups, who will be reminded of malted milk shakes and their favorite childhood candies. You are likely to find yourself giving out this recipe, or receiving requests for the brownies at every potluck and bake sale in your future.

1 TO 2 TABLESPOONS MELTED UNSALTED BUTTER, FOR THE BAKING DISH

1 CUP ALL-PURPOSE FLOUR

1 CUP MALTED MILK POWDER (SUCH AS OVALTINE MALT OR CARNATION MALTED MILK)

¼ CUP UNSWEETENED COCOA POWDER

¼ TEASPOON BAKING POWDER

½ TEASPOON SALT

8 OUNCES UNSWEETENED CHOCOLATE, CHOPPED

½ POUND (2 STICKS) UNSALTED BUTTER

1 CUP GRANULATED SUGAR

1 CUP DARK BROWN SUGAR, PACKED

1 TEASPOON VANILLA EXTRACT

4 LARGE EGGS, LIGHTLY BEATEN

1½ CUPS WHOLE MALTED MILK BALLS

Preheat the oven to 300°F. Brush a 9-by-13-inch baking pan with the melted butter and line the bottom with parchment paper. Set aside.

Sift together the flour, malted milk powder, cocoa powder, baking powder, and salt and set aside.

Melt the chocolate with the butter in a medium saucepan over low heat, stirring frequently. Transfer the chocolate mixture to a large bowl.

Stir the granulated sugar and the dark brown sugar into the chocolate mixture, using a wooden spoon. Add the vanilla and eggs and mix well. Stir in the flour mixture until just incorporated. Let the batter cool for 5 minutes.

continued

Fold the malted milk balls into the batter. Pour the batter into the prepared pan. Spread with a spatula to distribute the batter and malted milk balls evenly. Bake until the center is firm and the surface looks dry, about 45 minutes, turning the pan around after 30 minutes. Let the brownies cool completely in the pan.

When you're ready to serve, cut the brownies into squares.

TEN GREAT
ASSEMBLED DESSERTS

1. PEACH MELBA. For each serving, slice **1 peach** into thin wedges, put in a bowl or glass, and sprinkle with **1 teaspoon sugar** and **1 teaspoon freshly squeezed lemon juice.** Let sit for 5 minutes. Top with **a scoop of vanilla ice cream** and **a handful of raspberries.**

2. GREEK YOGURT PARFAIT. Place **1 cup dried apricots** and **½ cup dried sour cherries** in a saucepan, add **1 tablespoon honey,** and pour in enough **dry red wine** to cover. Simmer until the fruit is plump and most of the liquid is gone. Let the fruit cool, then spoon it over **thick Greek yogurt** in a pretty goblet or tumbler and top with **toasted walnut halves.** This sauce makes enough for 4 servings.

3. GLAZED FIGS. Slice **figs** lengthwise in half, sprinkle with **dark brown sugar,** and broil to melt the sugar and warm the fruit. Melt **raspberry jam** in a small saucepan or in the microwave, adding a tablespoon or two of water if needed to create a sauce. Place **a dollop of ricotta cheese** on each plate, arrange the figs alongside, and drizzle with the sauce.

4. GELATO WITH CHOCOLATE GANACHE. Bring **¼ cup heavy cream** to a boil and pour it over **3 ounces semisweet chocolate, finely chopped,** in a bowl. Stir until smooth. Spoon over **gelato,** and serve with **biscotti.** This sauce makes enough for 4 servings.

5. AFFOGATO. Serve bowls of vanilla or dulce de leche ice cream with a double shot of hot espresso on the side to pour over. Eat immediately.

6. AMBROSIA TRIFLE. Slice **angel food cake** and toast in a 400°F oven until golden. Peel and cut **1 orange** into sections. In a 350°F oven, toast **shredded coconut** until golden and **pecans** until fragrant. Sweeten **crème fraîche** to taste with **confectioners' sugar.** Layer the ingredients in clear dessert glasses. (These can be assembled in advance and stored in the fridge.)

7. FRESH APRICOTS WITH MASCARPONE.

Combine **1 teaspoon unsalted butter** and **1 tablespoon sugar** in a small frying pan and set over high heat. Cook for 2 minutes, swirling. Add **1 halved fresh apricot,** cut side down, and **1 teaspoon lemon juice** to the pan and reduce the heat slightly. Cook for 2 minutes on each side and transfer to a plate to cool slightly. Serve with **a dollop of mascarpone** and **3 to 4 crumbled mini amaretti cookies.**

8. SAUTÉED BANANAS WITH CARAMEL SAUCE.

Slice **2 bananas** into ¾-inch rounds. Sauté in **1 tablespoon unsalted butter** with **1 tablespoon light brown sugar** until glazed and brown. Serve over **vanilla ice cream,** with store-bought **caramel sauce.**

9. ICE CREAM SANDWICHES.

For each sandwich, place **a scoop of ice cream** on **a chocolate chip cookie** (try Tate's brand or another thin, crisp cookie). Top with **another cookie** and press down gently. Place on a rimmed baking sheet and set in the freezer. Wrap individually after they've hardened, and freeze until ready to serve.

10. NUTELLA SANDWICHES.

Toast **thinly sliced brioche bread,** spread with **Nutella,** and sprinkle with **confectioners' sugar.** Serve warm.

MERINGUE-SORBET LAYER CAKE

SERVES 6 TO 8

You don't need to bake this cake; it can be assembled with store-bought ingredients to make a fruity and crunchy layered dessert. Use three sorbet flavors that go well together, such as coconut, passion fruit, and raspberry. You can find the little meringue cookies in most good grocery stores; they're usually sold in plastic tubs in the bakery section.

5 CUPS CRUSHED MERINGUE COOKIES
(ABOUT 35)

3 PINTS FRUIT SORBET
(OF COMPLEMENTARY FLAVORS),
SOFTENED

WHIPPED CREAM, FOR SERVING
(OPTIONAL)

Line an 8-inch springform pan with enough plastic wrap to create an ample overhang. Use heavy-duty aluminum foil to build a collar inside the pan at the top, making the pan taller by 2 inches.

Sprinkle 1¼ cups of the crushed meringue cookies into the bottom of the pan. Spread 1 pint of the sorbet evenly over the meringue layer, making sure to reach the edges. Repeat these steps twice to make 3 layers, using 2 more pints of sorbet (use a different sorbet flavor for each layer) and an additional 2½ cups of the crushed cookies. Top the cake with the remaining 1¼ cups crushed cookies.

Cover the cake with the overhanging plastic wrap and freeze until ready to serve. When ready to serve, remove the outer ring of the springform, remove the foil collar and the plastic wrap, and transfer the cake to a serving plate. Let soften for 10 minutes, slice into wedges, and serve with whipped cream, if desired.

MAKE-AHEAD CHOCOLATE SOUFFLÉS

SERVES 8

Making soufflés is no more complicated than mixing up any cake batter, and they can be made a day or two ahead and popped into the oven a half hour before serving. These roux-based soufflés won't fall as fast as pastry-cream-based soufflés would, and even if they do, they're still good, very similar to a flourless chocolate cake (make a few extra and enjoy the next day). Fill individual baking dishes three-quarters full, no matter what their size.

1 TABLESPOON UNSALTED BUTTER, PLUS MORE FOR BUTTERING THE RAMEKINS

⅓ CUP SUGAR, PLUS MORE FOR COATING THE RAMEKINS

8 OUNCES BITTERSWEET CHOCOLATE, CHOPPED

1 TABLESPOON ALL-PURPOSE FLOUR

½ CUP MILK

3 LARGE EGGS, YOLKS AND WHITES SEPARATED, PLUS 2 LARGE EGG WHITES (SAVE THE 2 YOLKS FOR ANOTHER USE)

1 TEASPOON VANILLA EXTRACT

CREAM OF TARTAR

Preheat the oven to 375°F. Butter eight 6-ounce ovenproof ramekins and coat the bottom and insides with sugar; tap out excess sugar.

Melt the chocolate in a double boiler over simmering water. Transfer to a large bowl.

In a small saucepan, melt the 1 tablespoon butter. Add the flour and cook, stirring constantly, for 1 to 2 minutes, until thickened. Gradually add the milk and cook, whisking briskly, until thickened. Remove the saucepan from the heat and whisk in the 3 egg yolks and the vanilla. Pour the milk mixture over the chocolate and whisk until blended. Set aside.

Using a handheld mixer or a stand mixer, beat the 5 egg whites with a pinch of cream of tartar until they form soft peaks. Gradually add the ⅓ cup sugar and beat on high speed until the egg whites are stiff and shiny but not dry.

Use a rubber spatula to fold the egg whites into the chocolate mixture in batches. Divide the mixture evenly among the ramekins, filling them about three-quarters full. (At this point, the soufflés can be refrigerated, covered, for 1 to 2 days until you are ready to bake them.) Run your thumb around the edge of the dishes right before baking so that nothing will hinder an even rise, and to get that nice top-hat look to your finished soufflés.

Put the soufflés on a rimmed baking sheet and bake for 15 to 17 minutes, until the tops are cracked and the soufflés have risen but the centers are still molten. Serve immediately.

RESOURCES

Specialized Ingredients

Despaña
408 Broome Street
New York, NY 10013
212-219-5050
despanabrandfoods.com
For Spanish cheeses, meats,
and olives.

Dufour Pastry Kitchens
251 Locust Avenue
Bronx, NY 10454
800-439-1282
dufourpastrykitchens.com
For puff pastry dough.

Ideal Cheese
942 First Avenue
New York, NY 10022
212-688-7579
800-382-0109
idealcheese.com
For specialty cheeses.

Lamazou
370 Third Avenue
New York, NY 10016
212-532-2009
lamazoucheese.com
For specialty cheeses and meats.

Murray's Cheese Shop
254 Bleecker Street
New York, NY 10014
212-243-3289
murrayscheese.com
For specialty cheeses.

Niman Ranch
1350 South Loop Road, Suite 120
Alameda, CA 94502
nimanranch.com
For bone-in whole hams.

Russ and Daughters
179 East Houston Street
New York, NY 10002
212-475-4880
800-RUSS-289
russanddaughters.com
For smoked salmon and "appetizing."

Kitchen Tools and Equipment

Didrik's
190 Concord Avenue
Cambridge, MA 02138
617-354-5700
800-833-7505
didriks.com
For Libeco aprons, table linens,
glassware, and flatware.

Macy's
800-289-6229
macys.com
For chafing dishes, warming trays, and other serveware.

Sur La Table
800-243-0852
surlatable.com
For kitchen must-haves: cast-iron skillet, enameled Dutch oven, immersion blender, kitchen tongs, fish spatula, instant-read thermometer, offset spatula, Microplane grater, Japanese mandoline, and more.

Williams-Sonoma
877-812-6235
williams-sonoma.com
For kitchen must-haves: cast-iron skillet, enameled Dutch oven, immersion blender, kitchen tongs, fish spatula, instant-read thermometer, offset spatula, Microplane grater, Japanese mandoline, and more.

Serving and Party Supplies

ABC Carpet & Home
888 & 881 Broadway
New York, NY 10003
212-473-3000
abchome.com
For platters, serving bowls, and woodenware.

CB2
800-606-6252
cb2.com
For plates and dinnerware.

West Elm
888-922-4119
westelm.com
For platters and serving bowls.

INDEX

CONVERSION CHARTS

Here are rounded-off equivalents between the metric system and the traditional systems that are used in the United States to measure weight and volume.

FRACTIONS	DECIMALS
⅛	.125
¼	.25
⅓	.33
⅜	.375
½	.5
⅝	.625
⅔	.67
¾	.75
⅞	.875

WEIGHTS

US/UK	METRIC
¼ oz	7 g
½ oz	15 g
1 oz	30 g
2 oz	55 g
3 oz	85 g
4 oz	110 g
5 oz	140 g
6 oz	170 g
7 oz	200 g
8 oz (½ lb)	225 g
9 oz	250 g
10 oz	280 g
11 oz	310 g
12 oz	340 g
13 oz	370 g
14 oz	400 g
15 oz	425 g
16 oz (1 lb)	455 g

VOLUME

AMERICAN	IMPERIAL	METRIC
¼ tsp		1.25 ml
½ tsp		2.5 ml
1 tsp		5 ml
½ Tbsp (1½ tsp)		7.5 ml
1 Tbsp (3 tsp)		15 ml
¼ cup (4 Tbsp)	2 fl oz	60 ml
⅓ cup (5 Tbsp)	2½ fl oz	75 ml
½ cup (8 Tbsp)	4 fl oz	125 ml
⅔ cup (10 Tbsp)	5 fl oz	150 ml
¾ cup (12 Tbsp)	6 fl oz	175 ml
1 cup (16 Tbsp)	8 fl oz	250 ml
1¼ cups	10 fl oz	300 ml
1½ cups	12 fl oz	350 ml
2 cups (1 pint)	16 fl oz	500 ml
2½ cups	20 fl oz (1 pint)	625 ml
5 cups	40 fl oz (1 qt)	1.25 l

OVEN TEMPERATURES

	°F	°C	GAS MARK
very cool	250–275	130–140	½–1
cool	300	148	2
warm	325	163	3
moderate	350	177	4
moderately hot	375–400	190–204	5–6
hot	425	218	7
very hot	450–475	232–245	8–9

°C/F TO °F/C CONVERSION CHART

°C/F	°C	°F	°C/F	°C	°F	°C/F	°C	°F	°C/F	°C	°F
90	32	194	220	104	428	350	177	662	480	249	896
100	38	212	230	110	446	360	182	680	490	254	914
110	43	230	240	116	464	370	188	698	500	260	932
120	49	248	250	121	482	380	193	716	510	266	950
130	54	266	260	127	500	390	199	734	520	271	968
140	60	284	270	132	518	400	204	752	530	277	986
150	66	302	280	138	536	410	210	770	540	282	1,004
160	71	320	290	143	554	420	216	788	550	288	1,022
170	77	338	300	149	572	430	221	806			
180	82	356	310	154	590	440	227	824			
190	88	374	320	160	608	450	232	842			
200	93	392	330	166	626	460	238	860			
210	99	410	340	171	644	470	243	878			

Example: If your temperature is 90°F, your conversion is 32°C; if your temperature is 90°C, your conversion is 194°F.

17 Dec 11
B+T
12.95 (7.06)

Copyright © 2013, 2017 by Susan Spungen
Photographs copyright © 2017 by Lauren Volo
Illustrations copyright © 2013 by Sun Young Park

Library of Congress Cataloging-in-Publication Data

Names: Spungen, Susan, author.
Title: The artisanal kitchen. Party food / Susan Spungen.
Other titles: Party food
Description: New York, NY : Artisan, a division of Workman Publishing Co., Inc. [2017] | Includes bibliographical references and index.
Identifiers: LCCN 2017009973 | ISBN 9781579658052 (paper-over-board)
Subjects: LCSH: Entertaining. | Holiday cooking. | LCGFT: Cookbooks.
Classification: LCC TX731 .S6839 2017 | DDC 642/.4—dc23
LC record available at https://lccn.loc.gov/2017009973

Cover design by Erica Heitman-Ford
Cover photographs by Lauren Volo
Design by Erica Heitman-Ford

Artisan books are available at special discounts when purchased in bulk for premiums and sales promotions as well as for fund-raising or educational use. Special editions or book excerpts also can be created to specification. For details, contact the Special Sales Director at the address below, or send an e-mail to specialmarkets@workman.com.

Published by Artisan
A division of Workman Publishing Co., Inc.
225 Varick Street
New York, NY 10014-4381
artisanbooks.com

Artisan is a registered trademark of Workman Publishing Co. Inc.

This book has been adapted from *What's a Hostess to Do?* by Susan Spungen (Artisan, 2013).

Published simultaneously in Canada by Thomas Allen & Son, Limited

Printed in China

First printing, September 2017

10 9 8 7 6 5 4 3 2 1